MASTER YOUR LEARNING

A PRACTICAL GUIDE TO LEARN MORE DEEPLY,
RETAIN INFORMATION LONGER AND BECOME
A LIFELONG LEARNER

THIBAUT MEURISSE

CONTENTS

INTRODUCTION

 We now accept the fact that learning is a lifelong process of keeping abreast of change. And the most pressing task is to teach people how to learn.

— PETER DRUCKER, MANAGEMENT CONSULTANT.

In many aspects, learning is a natural process. As human beings, we are highly adaptive creatures able to learn anything we need to ensure our survival. Yet, nowadays, the world has become more complex. While learning is more important than ever, it is also more complicated - and often much more abstract.

Many people struggle to find the exact information they need to reach their learning goals, let alone understand things at a deep enough level to remember them.

This is where I'm supposed to tell you that I'm a far better learner than you. Unfortunately, that is not the case. When I began my research to write this book, I read an entire book on learning in a couple of sittings. A few weeks later, when I took a piece of paper and wrote down everything I could remember, I'm ashamed to admit it wasn't much. I found it impossible to remember even one specific

v

thing from the book. After a few minutes staring at a blank page, I gave up. Then, I looked at the book's Table of Contents, hoping it would jog my memory. It did, but only marginally.

Although I had spent hours reading the book, I couldn't recall the structure, the main ideas, or the concepts. Sure, since I had prior knowledge about the topic, I could deduce some of the points covered, but I couldn't remember anything specific. Nor could I recall a concrete example.

Does this sound familiar?

Now, reading a book only takes a few hours, but what about spending years sitting at a desk for hours every day? That is, what about school? How much do you remember from all those years spent studying at school? If you had to write down everything you remembered from primary school, junior high school, high school, or even university, how much could you recall?

The truth is, eventually, we will forget most of the things we learn. And it is not a bad thing. In many aspects, we can say that learning is about forgetting—forgetting the unnecessary things so that we can remember a minority of things that are truly important to us.

Contrary to popular belief, your brain isn't designed to remember everything you've ever heard, felt, smelled, tasted or touched. Sure, I *could* tell you that your subconscious is powerful almost beyond limit, but will it help you become an effective learner? I doubt it. I also won't tell you how to triple your reading speed and read a book in a day. Information overload is one of the main reasons people struggle to learn effectively.

Today, we are constantly incentivized to consume more information. Meanwhile, we fail to spend enough time and effort to build the strong foundations of learning. In the absence of solid foundations, we have nothing on which to build additional knowledge. As a result, major concepts, laws or theories are drowned under a sea of random facts, useless statistics or irrelevant stories.

Sadly, before we've had time to digest information, we find ourselves already having jumped onto the next book or video. While these efforts give us the illusion we're gaining knowledge, it couldn't be further from the truth. At best, we're accumulating facts, not knowledge; let alone wisdom.

When it comes to learning, the issue isn't poor memory, slow reading or lack of information; it is failing to identify the most *relevant* information, and failing to encode it properly so that we can learn and remember.

In this book, we'll see how you can alter your approach to learning and become a truly effective learner.

In **Part I. Building Solid Learning Roots**, I'll provide you with the key components needed to foster effective learning. We'll review major misconceptions and discuss what learning actually is. I'll also introduce six common learning challenges. In addition, we'll see how you can develop a powerful mindset that will help you learn anything you desire. Finally, I'll show you how to prioritize your learning to produce optimal results.

By the end of **Part I**, you'll have developed the four pillars required to begin growing your learning tree. That is, you will have:

- Built a solid understanding of how learning works (awareness),
- Developed a powerful learning mindset (mindset),
- Identified what you should learn and in what order (clarity), and
- Created an effective action plan (strategy).

Armed with solid awareness, a proper mindset, deep clarity and a sound strategy, you'll be ready to move onto **Part II**.

In **Part II. Strengthening Your Learning Tree Trunk**, we'll discuss the importance of building solid foundations. We'll see why you must dedicate more time and effort to studying core concepts, major principles, principal laws and theories, as well as fundamental techniques. This part is all about building a solid knowledge trunk on top of which you'll be able to add further knowledge.

In **Part III. Watering Your Tree**, we'll work on creating the necessary conditions for your tree to grow even taller and stronger. We'll review the most effective techniques you can use to learn better and to retain more information. You'll discover that effective learning is mostly about making a conscious effort to recall information multiple times at spaced intervals. Armed with effective learning techniques, you'll give your learning tree all the water and nutrients it needs to grow.

In **Part IV. Pruning Your Tree**, we'll see how to prune unnecessary branches to ensure your tree is as strong as it can be. We'll discuss issues such as information overload or the Shiny Object Syndrome. When you consume too much information, you keep adding branches to a weakened and overstressed trunk (i.e., you have weak foundations). As a result, you're left with a bunch of facts, stories, historical dates or sub-concepts that you can't do anything with. This leads to many issues which we'll explore in this part.

Finally, in **Part V. The Four Different Types of Learning**, we'll explain in detail four different types of learning: conceptual learning, practical skills, language learning and standardized tests. We'll see what each of these types is and how to best approach them. You'll also be provided with all the resources you'll need to help you become an effective learner in each learning type.

Let's get started, shall we?

Master Your Life With The Mastery Series

This book is the ninth book in the *Mastery Series*. You can check out the first book, *Master Your Emotions* at the URL below:

http://mybook.to/Master_Emotions

What readers say about *Master Your Emotions*:

"I am a psychologist and I love this book because of it's simplicity. It is so easy to read and understand. I will be referring many of my clients to download this book." -- Laura Beth Cooper, Ph.D., Psychologist

"Changed my life"

"This book kept me all the way to the end! I couldn't put it down and when I did I couldn't wait to pick it up again!"

"One of the best self help books I have ever read!"

"This will be one of my go to books, like How to Win Friends and Influence People, Start with Why, and a handful of others that I will continuously go back to."

Your free step-by-step action guide

To help you master your learning, I've created an action guide as a companion to this book. I highly encourage you to download it at the following URL:

https://whatispersonaldevelopment.org/master-your-learning

If you have any difficulties downloading the action guide, contact me at

thibaut.meurisse@gmail.com,

and I will send it to you as soon as possible.

PART I

BUILDING SOLID
LEARNING ROOTS

1

WHY LEARNING IS IMPORTANT

Learning is natural, though some people are much more deliberate learners than others. Why does this matter? Why should you care about becoming a more effective learner?

In this section, we'll briefly review the main reasons why learning is so critical. This will set the tone for the rest of the book.

A. Learning is the ultimate goal-achieving process

Many people fail to realize that learning is much more than remembering the contents of a book or mastering a skill. Here is one definition of learning I encourage you to reflect on:

Learning is the process that enables you to move from where you are to where you want to be.

Think about that for a moment. Why aren't you already where you want to be in certain areas of your life? One of the main reasons is that you still have lessons to learn. If you already knew everything and already had all the skills and qualities necessary to reach your goals, you would likely have attained them. Right?

This is why learning is fundamental. It's not just about cramming information into your head the night before an exam, or absorbing cool facts to impress your friends. Learning is the process that enables you to become the person you aspire to be.

B. Learning is power on demand

Whoever knows how to learn effectively has an extraordinary power. Why? Because, in a world where we are just a few clicks away from all the information we need, knowing how to use that information to learn anything we want will enable us to achieve almost any goal.

C. Learning acts as a powerful safety net

You can be stripped of all your money and possessions, but nobody can take away your ability to learn. Once you know how to think well, filter out unnecessary or erroneous information, create an effective action plan and implement it ruthlessly, you can use that skill to learn anything you wish. And, in a fast-changing world, this skill will become increasingly valuable moving forward.

D. Learning is humbling

As a rule of thumb, the more ready you are to let go of your ego, the faster you will learn. Most people refrain from asking for help in case it makes them look stupid. They're afraid of being ridiculed, appearing weak or being seen as incapable. Unfortunately, this is precisely what prevents them from learning. Instead of trying to be right or look good, see yourself as a learner. Connect your identity and sense of confidence with your ability to make mistakes and learn. When you are driven by how much you can learn, you'll inevitably become a far more effective learner.

I hope you're now convinced by the importance of true learning.

2
___

HOW GOOD OF A LEARNER ARE YOU?

Before we discuss the main misconceptions and issues related to learning, let's see how effective a learner you are. To do this, rate yourself on a scale from 1 to 10 for each of the statements below (where 1 is mostly false and 10 is mostly true):

- I often get lost in the sea of information available to me.
- Having a strong desire to learn, I often consume too much content too quickly, without using active learning techniques like recall.
- I read and reread the same textbooks without making a conscious effort to recall what I've read.
- When thinking of how far I am from reaching my goals, I feel discouraged or overwhelmed.
- I often put off doing important tasks that would allow me to make tangible progress toward my goals.
- I learn a lot of things but never master any of them.
- I forget most of what I read even when the topic genuinely interests me.
- I often remember insignificant details, facts or statistics, while losing track of the big picture.
- I assume that because I read a lot about a topic, I know it

very well (i.e., I believe I'm more knowledgeable than I really am).

- I often study things I'm not really interested in or curious about, and I do so to please others or to look cool.

If you scored high, it's great news. It means you have loads of room to improve your learning skills. Many of the issues noted above are common concerns. As you read this book, you'll learn to tackle them and become a more effective learner.

EIGHT MISCONCEPTIONS ABOUT LEARNING

Have you ever thought along these lines?

"I have a terrible memory." "If only I could read faster." "I wish I could understand things more effortlessly."

Who hasn't ever dreamed of being able to read something once and remember it forever? Unfortunately, that's not realistic. Forgetting is a normal part of the learning process.

The problem with having unrealistic expectations or misconceptions is that they can lead to a sense of demotivation. We start thinking that we aren't good enough to learn the skills we need to reach our goals. Or we believe things should come more quickly and easily. Consequently, we look for a magic pill and end up jumping from one new concept to the next. Then, when nothing seems to work, we become discouraged and give up.

Fortunately, as you let go of your misconceptions, you'll be less likely to give up on your goals and, as a result, learning will come more easily to you.

Now, let's review eight main misconceptions of learning. For each misconception, reflect on how it may apply to your specific situation.

Misconception #1: I need more information

 The number of books completed is a vanity metric. As you know more, you leave more books unfinished.

— NAVAL RAVIKANT, ENTREPRENEUR AND INVESTOR.

In today's consumer society, "more" seems to be the answer to all our problems. The tenet suggests that we need to consume more information to help us reach our professional or personal goals. But is that so?

Every day, we consume a staggering amount of information. Do we really need to consume more? The truth is, you probably need to consume *less*, but this must be much more *targeted* information. That is, what you learn should be more strategically aligned with your overall goals. The more clarity you have, the easier it will be to eliminate unnecessary information and focus strictly on what you need.

Later in this book, we'll see how you can clarify your learning goals. For now, remember that when it comes to learning, less information is often more.

Misconception #2: I need to learn faster

 In any event, the speed at which they read, be it fast or slow, is but a fractional part of most people's problem with reading.

— MORTIMER J. ADLER, AUTHOR OF, *HOW TO READ A BOOK*.

There is nothing wrong with learning faster. But trying to learn more than you can absorb is counterproductive. For instance, doubling or tripling your reading speed won't necessarily make you a better learner. It probably won't improve your understanding of the material or your ability to retain it. Why? Because it's masking the symptom (slow reading) rather than addressing the root cause (poor understanding). As you become more knowledgeable in a field, you'll grasp more concepts and improve your understanding. As a result, when you read relevant material, your reading speed will increase naturally.

For instance, I've read hundreds of personal-development-related books in English. This is why, even though English isn't my mother tongue, I can read fairly quickly and with ease.

However, you can't speed-read out of nowhere when you have little or no understanding of a topic or when you lack the correct vocabulary. Think of it as learning a foreign language. I could probably speed-read in Italian—but since I don't speak Italian, how could I possibly understand what I'm reading?

Also, note that *understanding* something doesn't mean you'll retain it over the long term. As I've already said, I once read an entire book from cover to cover but, a few weeks later, I couldn't remember anything about it.

Misconception #3: My memory sucks

 Being a student is easy. Learning requires actual work.

— WILLIAM CRAWFORD, POLITICIAN.

While it's true that some people have a better memory than others, memory is usually not the key issue when it comes to learning. If anything, it is a symptom that shows your learning strategies are inadequate. In other words, you don't struggle with learning because you have a poor memory; you have a poor memory because of an ineffective approach to learning. By changing your approach, you'll be able to retain much more information and retain it more readily.

Misconception #4: I must remember as much as possible

 Any fool can know. The point is to understand.

— ALBERT EINSTEIN, PHYSICIST.

If you believe your subconscious is a powerful tool that can remember everything, you'll expect yourself to remember a lot of what you read, listen to, watch or do. However, forgetting is not only inevitable, but it's also necessary. The key question is not "How can I remember as much as possible?", but "What should I strive to remember, and what can, or should I forget?"

For instance, if you tend to forget side stories or statistics, perhaps you shouldn't make any effort to commit them to long-term memory. If you *do* want to remember them, you should make an extra effort to do so by taking notes, highlighting key sentences, et cetera.

Therefore, beware if you hold the assumption that you should remember as much as you can. It will restrict your ability to learn.

Misconception #5: Each piece of information is made equal

 When it comes to reading, make sure your foundation is very, very high quality.

— NAVAL RAVIKANT, ENTREPRENEUR AND INVESTOR.

The quality of the information you consume varies greatly. Some books, lectures or articles have the potential to change your life, while others are irrelevant or useless. However, do you act accordingly? Do you spend enough time consuming high-quality information, rereading valuable books until you squeeze every drop of knowledge out of them? Or do you read them once and discard them as you would do with low-quality books?

It may be unconscious, but most of us haven't learned to sort information effectively. Part of this challenge may relate to the way we learned at school, where we weren't taught to prioritize information. Instead, we merely studied what we were told to study.

As a result, we now read books we probably shouldn't, watch videos that teach us nothing and take courses on topics we don't deeply care about. This inability to organize information based on its quality and usefulness leads to several key issues, such as:

- Information overload
- Analysis paralysis, and
- Poor retention

We'll elaborate on these issues in the next section, "Six common learning issues".

In truth, it might be more effective to spend several months absorbing the contents of one great book rather than reading twenty mediocre books superficially.

The writer and mathematician, Nassim Taleb, identifies how long a book has been in print before reading it. For him, if a book hasn't been around for at least ten or twenty years, it's probably not worth reading. Things that stand the test of time generally do so for a reason.

The point is, if you find yourself reading too many books, consider narrowing your choice to "proven" books, and delve deeper with them. This will reduce the risk of coming across low-quality information.

Remember, information isn't made equal. Learn to discriminate between mediocre and high-quality material. Then, consume less information but make sure what you do consume it is of a higher quality and relevancy.

Misconception #6: I need to finish what I started reading

 Wisdom is learning what to overlook.

— WILLIAM JAMES, PHILOSOPHER AND PSYCHOLOGIST.

This point is related to the previous one. In the same way we've been taught to finish the food on our plates, we've been conditioned to read books or articles until the end. Again, this is not always something we're necessarily conscious of doing. To become an effective learner, you must practice analyzing every piece of information you come across to determine whether it is worth your time. The point is this. You don't always need to finish what you're reading—this book being an obvious exception.

The venture capitalist and philosopher, Naval Ravikant, perceives books as, "throwaway blog posts or bite-sized tweets or posts." He doesn't feel obliged to finish any book he starts. I'm not saying it's the best learning strategy, but when you're looking for a specific piece of information or want to get a basic overview, this might be a good idea under specific circumstances.

Misconception #7: I can recognize it therefore I know it

 It's what you learn after you know it all that counts.

— HARRY S TRUMAN, 33RD PRESIDENT OF THE UNITED STATES.

When it comes to learning, we must differentiate between recognition and retrieval. For example, you may read a textbook several times, but it doesn't indicate you've learned much. It can help you answer multiple-choice questions correctly (recognition), but it doesn't necessarily mean you can recall the contents of the textbook in the absence of any clue (retrieval). And just because you can recall its contents today doesn't mean you'll be able to recall it next week, let alone next month or next year.

The bottom line is this: just because you feel you're learning doesn't mean you actually are. Here is a good rule of thumb: the less effort you exert—reading a book passively, watching a video while doing something else, et cetera—the less you're really learning. Inversely, the more effort you make—taking notes using your own words, summarizing the content in your head, recalling key concepts, et cetera—the more you're learning.

Misconception #8: I need to learn X, Y or Z

 Study without desire spoils the memory, and it retains nothing that it takes in.

— LEONARDO DA VINCI, SCIENTIST, ARTIST AND INVENTOR.

What are you currently learning and why? You may often learn things you shouldn't. You might do so to be like everybody else or to appear smarter. For instance, you may decide that it would be nice to speak a foreign language, dance the salsa or know how to bake cakes, but if you have no genuine desire to learn, you'll most likely give up. And even if you manage to study consistently for a while, over time, you'll probably end up forgetting most of what you've learned.

Therefore, make sure you learn something because you *really* want to, or you absolutely must. Before you commit to learning anything, give yourself time to think it through. Then, after a few weeks, if you still want to learn it, consider getting started. Avoid focusing on what you *need* to learn. Instead, focus on what you *want* to learn.

These are some of the main misconceptions people have. How many of them can you relate to?

Now, let's discuss what the process we call "learning" is actually about.

4

WHAT LEARNING IS

Have you ever considered what the learning process is really about? Writing this book gave me the opportunity to reflect on this question. In this section, I'll share with you the key components of effective learning. Once you understand what learning is about, you'll be able to change your approach and learn more effectively.

Learning is becoming a better thinker

In many aspects, learning is about becoming a better thinker. This is because to acquire knowledge you must be able to:

- Approach your learning thoughtfully to ensure that it is effective and aligned with your goals, values and topics of interest
- Filter out the irrelevant information to gather high-quality material that is relevant to your learning goals
- Ask yourself smart questions to extract the key points from any learning materials you encounter
- Encode core messages and important lessons in a way that facilitates learning and boost retention, and
- Use many different mental models to help you make better

decisions regarding your learning (e.g., what to learn, how to learn it, etc.)

Most of the points in this section are aimed at making you a better thinker, and as a result, a more effective learner.

Let's explore each one in turn.

A. Learning is turning chaos into order

Information has no value in and of itself, it's all about the context that surrounds it. For instance, the information "it will rain today" isn't of much value to us if we plan to stay at home, but for the farmer whose harvest depends on the weather, it's invaluable. The same goes for learning. A Japanese textbook for beginners isn't helpful to the advanced student, and an academic book on the history of learning isn't that relevant to me when my goal is to write a practical guide on the subject.

The point is, you must have a clear goal so that you know where to find the right information. By doing so, you can turn chaos (information overflow) into order (meaningful information that helps you reach your goal).

Below are a few tips to ensure the information is relevant:

- **Filter it based on your goals.** You must identify a clear goal so that you can gather the relevant information. Without a learning goal, you can't select the relevant information. Everything else is just noise. Context is everything.
- **Sort it out.** Identify the most valuable pieces of information. Without priority, all information weighs the same, which makes it impossible to skim through the sheer volume of knowledge available.
- **Use it to grab "big picture".** You must become better at grasping the big picture and identifying major concepts. Without a solid understanding of the key concepts, learning will quickly turn into an overwhelming process in which

useless facts, irrelevant stories, unimportant statistics and obscure concepts blend together.

The bottom line is that learning is a process of elimination that can only happen once you have a well-defined goal and a well-defined plan. Then, and only then, can you select the appropriate information to retain. This is what turning chaos into order means.

B. Learning is thinking well

On the surface, it may seem as though learning is all about remembering things. While this is true, we can't learn anything unless we store it somewhere in our brain. How we store the data is what matters most. Great learners remember things, not just because they have an excellent memory, but because of the way they process information—which results from their thinking process.

I couldn't remember anything a few weeks after reading a particular book, but is it because I have a poor memory? No—or only partially. It's because my thinking process wasn't conducive to enabling effective retention. That is, I had no specific goal in mind and failed to approach the material effectively. I bought into the myth that reading the book from cover to cover would be enough to retain the information I needed. Or perhaps I just didn't want to do the actual work of *learning*.

The point is, whether we're conscious of it or not, we approach learning material in a certain way—i.e., we entertain a specific thought process. This thought process may or may not be highly effective.

Now, what do I mean exactly by "thought process"?

I mean the cognitive process we rely on for learning, which includes:

1. The questions we ask ourselves before approaching any learning material, and
2. The way we interact with the material (i.e., pausing between paragraphs, looking for key concepts summarizing content, etc.)

Let's explore each of these points briefly.

1. Asking yourself questions

The better you become at asking relevant questions, the more effective your learning will be. The key is to define your learning goals and identify a few pertinent questions. Here are a few examples:

- What specific learning goal do I have in mind?
- What information am I looking for exactly?
- Why am I going through this learning material?
- What are the major questions I hope to answer by reading this material?
- What's the most relevant information for me here?
- Which parts of the material should I read and which parts should I skip?

The more you think before and during learning, the better quality information you'll be able to identify and absorb.

2. Interacting with the material

Learning doesn't happen passively. It is the result of your interaction with the learning materials. The better you become at interacting with the information, the more effective your learning will be. More specifically:

- Look at the overall structure. What's the main thesis stated by the author in the introduction? How is the book, lecture or article structured and why? Is the course or video relevant to you and your learning goals?
- Pause between paragraphs, and reread sentences you feel are important. Remember: all information isn't made equal. Some sentences will resonate with you; others won't.
- Summarize paragraphs or chapters in your head. Interacting with the material means reformulating it, using your own words. It helps you better understand what you read and increases your ability to retain it.

- Keep asking yourself what the most relevant information is. Most of the information you consume isn't that important to your goals. Be rigorous with the way you select information.
- Look for ways to connect what you read with what you already know. We often learn through the association of ideas. Therefore, strive to connect what you read with information you already have. What does it remind you of? What is it like? What personal examples could you use to illustrate new concepts?

To sum up, don't consume information passively, but have a conversation with the learning material. Good learners think well. With practice, they build an effective thought process that enables them to learn better.

C. Learning is building a library of concepts

Learning doesn't happen in a vacuum. It requires you to build a library of concepts. This is because the more concepts you know, the more nuances you can understand and the more knowledgeable you will become.

Think of concepts as receptacles of knowledge. The more concepts you know, the more knowledge you can fill them with. By building a vast library of concepts, you have a massive number of receptacles for learning that will enable you to make connections with new concepts more easily.

For instance, if you can't perform basic calculations, you won't be able to perform advanced calculus. Similarly, if you don't grasp basic concepts such as P/E ratio, discount cash flow or CAGR, you might struggle to understand anything that a financial analyst says. This is simply because you don't have a receptacle for such knowledge.

But what are concepts? I define concepts as meaningful chunks of information that help you organize new information more effectively, and as a result, facilitate your learning. For instance, concepts may be:

- **New words or expressions.** Words represent ideas. The greater your subject-specific vocabulary, the easier it is to learn (and remember). When you read a book on a technical topic you know nothing about, you'll have a hard time understanding, let alone remembering anything. You simply can't internalize what you do not understand. In this case, knowing more concepts and words is essential.
- **Facts.** Knowing facts creates a solid foundation on which you can base your thinking and learning. For instance, to learn history, you need to know what happened at certain historical dates to establish a chronology and organize your knowledge in a coherent way.
- **Theories/Laws.** Like facts, these create a foundation for your thinking. The more theories and laws you know, the more tools you can use to make sense of new information. For instance, you won't go far in the field of physics if you do not understand Newtonian physics, the law of thermodynamics or Ohm's law.

To sum up, on your learning journey, you will acquire key concepts on top of which you can build more knowledge. The more concepts you know, the more concepts you can learn and the more information you can absorb.

D. Learning is being radically honest with yourself

Being eager to learn, you may bite off more than you can chew. As a result, the new knowledge you seek won't stick. In other words, your foundations will be shaky, which will make learning new concepts ineffective.

To become an effective learner, you must be honest enough with yourself to acknowledge when you don't understand something well. In this case, you must be willing to return to the fundamentals and re-learn key concepts.

For instance, let's say you enjoy reading books or watching videos about economics. You may think you're fairly knowledgeable on the subject, but are you really? For instance, can you describe the concepts outlined below accurately?

- Inflation/deflation
- Monetary policy
- Fiscal policy
- Supply and demand
- Keynesianism
- Neoliberalism, or
- Capitalism

Chances are that you'll struggle to explain any of these concepts.

The bottom line is: delve deeper with key concepts or practice basic moves for any practical skills you seek to master. Think of martial arts experts. They practice the same move thousands upon thousands of times. They don't assume they know everything, and neither should you.

E. Learning is about building powerful mental models

Mental models are cognitive tools that help us to understand the world better and to navigate through it more effectively.

In a complex world with an ever-increasing volume of information available, mental models are vital tools that help us sort out information and make sense of the world. When our mental models are good, they enable us to make better decisions and achieve better results. Conversely, when our models are wildly inaccurate or inappropriate, they lead us to make poor decisions. The more effective mental models we internalize, the more tools we will have to deal with various life situations and the faster we'll learn. To sum up:

Effective mental models → better decisions → better learning strategies → better results.

Now, let me give you a few examples of mental models.

The 80/20 Principle

This mental model is based on real world observations. At the beginning of the twentieth century, Vilfredo Pareto, an Italian economist, noticed that, in Italy, twenty percent of the population owned eighty percent of the land. Later, this ratio has been shown to work in many different situations. For instance:

- Twenty percent of our actions often generate eighty percent of our results.
- Twenty percent of a company's clients often bring eighty percent of its profits.
- Twenty percent of a company's products often generate eighty percent of its sales.

When we apply this model to learning, we can assume the following things apply:

- Twenty percent of what you do generates eighty percent of your learning results.
- Twenty percent of the information you consume contains eighty percent of what you need to learn.
- Twenty percent of your learning habits leads to eighty percent of your learning.

The 80/20 Principle is probably one of the most powerful mental models out there. Make sure you use it as often as necessary.

Parkinson's Law

This law states that the amount of work expands to fill the time available for its completion. The more time you have, the longer you'll take to complete a task. That's why deadlines are powerful tools. Imagine what would happen in a world without deadlines. Most projects would never be completed, writers would spend years writing and rewriting, never finishing their books, and students would never complete their term papers. Understanding this business model can also help you learn faster and more effectively.

Note that the 80/20 Principle and Parkinson's Law can work well together, too. The less time you have available to finish something, the more you'll have to focus on the essential actions required to complete it (using the 80/20 Principle).

Newton's Law of Motion

According to this law, "An object either remains at rest or continues to move at a constant velocity, unless it is acted upon by an external force." This can also be an effective mental model when it comes to learning. For instance, if you implement a daily learning routine, you'll start building momentum, making slow and steady progress toward your goals. Conversely, when you have no routine (or fall off of your routine), you may experience resistance when trying to resume learning.

The above are just examples of how mental models work and how they can help you learn more effectively.

Ultimately, learning is about finding the right information and encoding it the right way. In this regard, mental models are helpful because they provide you with the tools to make better decisions and sharpen your thinking. And the better you think, the better you'll be able to learn.

F. Learning is discerning more nuances

Learning is akin to increasing the resolution of your computer screen. At low resolution, you only perceive the main concepts, which is rough and lacks granularity. But as you keep learning, the resolution improves. Now, you begin to see more detail. You notice the smallest nuance. You break down key concepts into sub-concepts, and as you grasp these sub-concepts more deeply, they give further room to allow in even more granular concepts.

For instance, think of chess players. The novice player only knows the basic rules and how to move each piece on the chessboard (low resolution). On the other hand, grandmasters have memorized tens of thousands of patterns (high resolution). With a simple glance, they can remember the location of all the pieces on the board. They can immediately spot different openings and think several moves ahead. Some highly skilled and gifted chess players can even play blindfolded against multiple opponents simultaneously.

Let me give you one more example. When I wrote my first book, I created a simple outline and started writing. I didn't think too much about it (low resolution) However, as I kept writing more books, I started grasping more nuances. I began to consider the rhythm of each sentence, paid extra attention to the coherence between each paragraph, avoided repeating the same words and so on. Over time, I've added dozens more criteria to my knowledge base. And with practice, I internalized them (high resolution).

Learning slows down time

As we gain more knowledge in our field, time starts slowing down— or so it seems. We can anticipate moves, think faster and produce more and better content than most people. Through consistent practice, we have transferred our skills to the subconscious. In other words, we've taken a difficult concept, an elaborate move or a complex process, and compacted it into one chunk of information and stored it in our minds.

To give a computing analogy, acquiring knowledge is like putting a large amount of information into a zip file. While experts can unzip the file instantly and with ease, beginners must process information in real-time, which requires significant effort.

The bottom line is that learning is discerning more nuances. Therefore, to improve your skills, increase your "resolution" by internalizing more concepts through practice.

G. Learning is doing

Oftentimes, people struggle to learn effectively because they perceive learning as a passive act, or they believe their subconscious will automatically absorb whatever information they come across. However, learning is an active process. The more active you are with your learning, the more effectively and efficiently you'll learn.

It is almost impossible to acquire true knowledge passively. Before something can become second nature to you—driving a car, delivering a flawless karate punch, giving an outstanding presentation, et cetera—you must make your brain work for it. Your subconscious can certainly help internalize knowledge and skills, but your conscious mind must do the heavy lifting first.

For example, many people believe that just by living in a foreign country they'll pick up the language, or that having a foreign boyfriend or girlfriend will magically make them fluent. Unfortunately, it doesn't work that way. It can help, of course, but you'll still have to put in the hard work.

Learning is doing. So, take action, and don't expect things to be easy.

SIX COMMON LEARNING ISSUES

Now that we've seen some of the biggest misconceptions around learning and have explained what learning is, let's delve into the most common learning challenges people face. As you proceed through this section, ask yourself how much each issue is relevant to your particular situation.

Issue #1: You try to learn too much

Most people try to learn more than they can accept. They keep reading books, watching videos or listening to podcasts without taking enough time to assimilate whatever it is they're trying to learn. Unfortunately, the brain cannot digest every piece of information we put into it.

By trying to absorb too much information, instead of ending up with more knowledge, we usually find ourselves confused. Our mind becomes disorganized, and we struggle to make sense of the countless books, videos, podcasts and articles we've accumulated over the years. On top of which, we probably retain little of what we learn.

I believe there are several reasons we fall prey to excessive learning, including:

1. **Lack of awareness.** Often, we're simply not aware that we are consuming too much information. It turns our mind into a junkyard full of useless bits of knowledge we don't know what to do with. While we may remember facts, statistics or stories, we fail to connect them in a coherent way, and we miss the big picture.

2. **Lack of clear goals.** In the absence of specific goals, we inevitably end up absorbing too much irrelevant information. Now, we don't have to consume every piece of information with a definite purpose in mind, but it's better if we have a few learning goals to help us filter out the redundant material.

3. **Insatiable desire to learn more.** If we love learning new things, it can become an addiction. Reading more books or listening to more podcasts gives us the illusion that we are learning and makes us feel good. For instance, it may give us a sense of superiority (we're learning more and are smarter than others). However, unless we take enough time to review what we're learning, we won't remember much.

What about you? Are you learning too much? It's okay if you are, since it means you have a strong desire to learn. The key is to structure your learning more effectively.

* * *

Action step

Using your action guide, write at least one specific time when you took on more than you could handle.

Issue #2: You're overly passive with your learning

This is one of the biggest problems people face. Here is the truth: learning is not a passive process. Let me repeat this: learning is *not* a passive process. It's an active process that requires effort—a great deal of effort. The reason you may forget most of what you learn is not that you have a poor memory, but that you're likely not learning in the correct way.

Let me share some examples of passive learning activities you may currently be engaging in:

- **Rereading the same passage over and over.** In most cases, rereading the same book will not help you retain the information better, it will only give you the *illusion* that you're learning. The content may start sounding familiar, but that doesn't mean you have mastered it.
- **Underlining sentences.** Underlining or highlighting is another way to make us feel we're actively learning. However, this has been shown to be rather ineffective.
- **Listening to podcasts/watching videos passively.** Passively consuming any type of information isn't an effective way to learn. There are better methods such as summarizing the content in your own words or trying to identify the main points in your head.
- **Cramming.** Cramming for an exam can certainly help you remember a lot of information over a short period, but you will probably forget most of what you learn quickly.

What about you? Are you a passive learner? What could you do specifically to turn yourself into an active learner?

* * *

Action step

Using your action guide, write down two to three concrete things you can start doing to become a more proactive learner.

Issue #3: There is no clear purpose behind your learning

In many aspects, we learn to gain skills that will allow us to move closer to the person we aspire to be. Yet, often, instead of learning what we really want to learn, we learn what we *think* we should learn (or what we're told to learn).

Sure, you may not always be able to learn the things that genuinely excite you, but that doesn't mean you shouldn't try. Many of the most successful people on the planet became the best at what they do because they're passionate about it. In fact, I would go as far as saying that passion alone is at least as powerful as all the other learning techniques you'll learn in this book. You could get all the learning techniques wrong and still master almost any skill if you have a strong enough passion for it, because you'll:

- Spend more time and dedicate more effort to learning it than almost anybody else,
- Retain information and learn much faster because you have a strong emotional connection to the learning materials, and
- Never give up even when you encounter challenges along the way (because you love the subject so much).

Like you, I'm on my journey to become a more effective learner. However, I still do a lot of things wrong and fall prey to most of the common issues mentioned in this section. Yet, despite inferior learning techniques, I was able to become a full-time writer without any writing degree and without even being a native English speaker. I learned how to write by following Stephen King's advice when he said, "If you want to be a writer, you must do two things above all others: read a lot and write a lot."

Similarly, in retrospect, I could have learned Japanese much more effectively, but because I loved studying Japanese and spent thousands upon thousands of hours studying it, I eventually became good at it.

The bottom line is you need to strive to learn things you genuinely want to learn. This will make your learning experience more enjoyable and more effective.

* * *

Action step

Using your action guide, list all the things you genuinely want to learn, not because you need to, or because you want to impress others, but because they really interest you.

Issue #4: You're not taking enough action

As we've already seen, you cannot learn without effort. Often, making an effort means taking action. Over the years, I have witnessed many people failing to reach their learning goals because they didn't take enough action. However, I have yet to find someone who failed because they took *too much* action. Now, here is what I mean by "taking action":

Doing the exact same thing you're trying to learn.

One key technique for effective learning is simply doing. If you want to become fluent in a foreign language, speak that language with a real person. If you want to become a competent driver, you must drive an actual car.

Common sense, right?

We'll talk about this tool in more detail in the section dedicated to effective learning tools.

* * *

Action step

Using your action guide, write down what taking more action would mean for you when it comes to learning.

Issue #5: You lack confidence in your ability to learn

Our belief in our ability to figure things out and learn anything we need to reach our goals determines how effectively we'll learn.

Personally, I'm not immune to lacking in confidence. In fact, I can clearly see that I'm still operating far below my true capabilities in most, if not all, areas of my life. The same goes for you and every other human being on the planet. The key question is, can you see how much more potential you have?

A lack of confidence in your ability to learn can manifest as follows:

- **Not making enough effort to learn.** Being afraid of finding out you aren't "good enough" or "smart enough", you'd rather not do your best. Because what if your best isn't enough? This scares you.
- **Procrastination.** Similarly, to avoid finding out whether you are smart enough, you continuously self-sabotage your learning. One way you do this is by doing something at the last moment to let you off the hook if the results aren't that good (i.e., "I could have done better if I had spent more time working on it").

Actually, I happen to engage in self-sabotaging behavior. I write less than I'd like to, I fail to take enough notes, I avoid practicing recalling what I've read, and do less research than I could. Fortunately, I have developed a mindset that enables me to keep moving forward with my learning and my long-term projects.

We'll discuss how to develop a proper mindset in greater depth in the next part. For now, remember that most of the things other people can learn, you can learn too. So, just for a moment, let go of any assumptions regarding what you can and cannot learn. Just focus on what you *really, really* want to learn. Remember, your level of excitement is one of the most powerful learning tools available to you.

Action step

If you could learn absolutely anything you desire, what would it be? Write down your answer in the action guide.

Issue #6: You have unrealistic expectations

Another common issue is believing you're learning when you aren't. It is often referred to as "the illusion of knowing". To learn effectively, you must be able to differentiate between "true" and "fake" learning.

Your learning journey is full of traps. You often assume you're learning more effectively than you are, and you believe you'll be able to recall more information than you do. This is an issue because it leads you to believe that something is wrong with you when reality crushes your expectations.

Below are some things to watch out for:

- Rereading the same passage or chapter
- Underlining passages, and
- Assuming you learn just because you understand the material

Remember, learning is an active process that requires effort. Because you seem to understand something doesn't mean you have actually learned it.

Action step

Using your action guide, write down specific situations when you fell for the illusion of knowing. In other words, write down things you don't know as well as you think.

Now, let's see how to develop a powerful mindset that will enable you to become a more effective learner.

6

DEVELOPING A LEARNING MINDSET

A. Shift your identity

Few people truly realize the power of identity and how malleable it is. Many people stay the same for most of their lives, never understanding that they could choose to transform their identity completely. If they were to do so, they would discover that things can dramatically improve for them.

I've experienced firsthand how powerful changing one's identity can be. My first major identity shift happened when I decided to impact millions of people with my work. I soon realized that the only way to do so was to see myself as a "high-performer". I needed to raise my standards so that I could fulfill my ambitious vision. How did I shift my identity?

I just decided to do it.

I decided that from a certain point onward, I was a top performer and would act like one. Then, I asked myself, what did it mean to perform at a high level? What did top performers do differently?

One of the answers was that high performers make promises to themselves and to others and keep them. As they do so consistently, they slowly but surely develop more confidence in their abilities. By achieving goals over and over, they come to believe they can reach bigger and bigger goals—and they succeed.

So, that's what I did. I set small goals and achieved them over and over. I implemented daily routines and stuck to them for months. Over time, I became a high performer.

Here is another example of an identity shift I undertook.

For years, when introducing myself, I would say, "I write books and sell them on Amazon." At some point, I realized I needed to shift from "I write books" to "I'm a writer". So, I started telling myself "I'm a writer" and visualized how I would introduce myself. Then, I moved from "I'm a writer" to an "I'm a six-figure author" identity. This became my daily mantra. Whenever I had to make a business-related decision, I would ask myself the following questions:

"As a six-figure author, can I afford not to do this?"

For instance, can I afford not to buy a course, test difference prices or write consistently?

The way you see yourself matters—a lot. Your identity will often become your reality—especially over a long period of time. You must see yourself as an incredible learner. You must believe in your ability to learn almost anything you desire. Identifying as a highly effective learner will completely transform your approach to learning. It will make you extremely resilient. It will help you enjoy the learning process more—even with all its ups and downs. And, as a result, it will enable you to acquire more skills and knowledge, enabling you to reach many of your goals.

Accordingly, if right now you see yourself as a poor learner, understand that it doesn't have to stay that way. Today, you can choose to wear the identity of a highly effective learner who refuses to quit. Imagine if you were guaranteed to learn anything you desired, how would you feel? How would it improve your life? What exciting new skills would you be able to learn?

Remember, learning is an inevitable process, why not make your learning more effective and efficient?

* * *

Action step

See yourself as a highly effective learner. To start building your new identity, complete the following sentence in your action guide. Create five to ten statements.

I'm an unstoppable learner, therefore I ...

B. Adopt a growth mindset

The fact that you're a learner isn't just a myth or something you say to make yourself feel better. Studies have shown that you can learn more effectively by altering your mindset (i.e., by moving from a *fixed* mindset to a *growth* mindset).

The concept of a growth mindset has been popularized by Carol Dweck in her book, *Mindset*. Having a growth mindset means understanding that you can become better and acting accordingly. It's realizing that your capacities aren't fixed, and you aren't destined to stay where you currently are for the rest of your life. People with a growth mindset believe their intelligence can grow, and they have a strong desire to learn. As a result, they will often:

- **Embrace challenges.** They understand that the only way to grow is by facing challenges. As a result, they welcome new challenges and believe in their ability to figure things out.
- **Persist in the face of obstacles.** They know they will have to work hard, and they will encounter many obstacles before they can reach their goals. The only way is through. Being honest with themselves and facing their inadequacies is a path they know they must take.
- **See effort as a path to mastery.** They perceive effort as necessary if they are to move toward mastery. They understand that success is a long-term process made of

peaks and valleys. Setbacks and disappointments are inevitable.

- **Accept constructive criticism.** We all have blind spots and weaknesses that we need to acknowledge and work on. Receiving constructive feedback—and perhaps, more importantly, acting on it no matter how uncomfortable it feels—is necessary. People with a growth mindset welcome constructive criticism. If they want to grow, this is one of the most effective tools they can use.
- **Learn from the success of others.** While they may sometimes feel jealous when seeing the success of other people around them, ultimately, they're determined to learn anything they can from successful people. They swallow their ego and look for ways to improve. They ask questions, return to the fundamentals, take extra classes and so on. They do not stop improving. They strive to become better at all costs.

On the other hand, people with a fixed mindset tend to believe that intelligence is static. As a result, they will often:

- **Try to look smart.** They fear being judged and looking dumb. As a result, they exert a tremendous amount of effort pretending to be smarter or more knowledgeable than they are, which prevents them from learning what they need to learn to move to the next level.
- **Avoid challenges.** Because they believe they aren't capable enough and are afraid of failing, they avoid challenging themselves.
- **Give up easily.** Not believing they can improve; they inevitably give up sooner rather than later.
- **See effort as pointless.** They give a task less than their best. Part of it is because if they were to give it everything they have and fail, it would be the ultimate proof they aren't smart enough. This scares them more than anything else, and since they believe their abilities are fixed, it means they can do

nothing about it. They'd much rather live in denial than try hard and still fail.

- **Ignore constructive criticism.** Any criticism is perceived as a threat to their ego. It confirms what they already "know": that they are not as good as they could be. And, again, since they don't believe they can improve, any feedback is pointless. It only hurts their feelings.

- **Feel threatened by the success of others.** To see how they fare, these people constantly compare themselves to others. They believe that success is limited and that, when others succeed, they're stealing their slice of the pie. Also, when people seem to be more successful than they are, it makes people with a fixed mindset feel inadequate, which confirms their biggest fears that they aren't good enough. As a result, they'd much rather surround themselves with less successful people.

What about you? Do you have a fixed mindset or a growth mindset?

Remember, you're an unstoppable learner, and the first step toward realizing your potential is to adopt a growth mindset. You can always learn. You can always grow. You can always improve. In fact, this is how your brain is designed.

* * *

Action step

Familiarize yourself with the following statements. They will help you build your new identity as an unstoppable learner.

- I embrace challenges
- I always persist in the face of obstacles
- I see effort as the necessary path to mastery
- I accept constructive criticism
- I learn from the success of others

Think of a goal you're pursuing right now. Using your action guide, write down concretely what would it mean for you to adopt a growth mindset to reach that goal.

C. Understand the power of neuroplasticity

For hundreds of years, it was thought that our brains were fixed and incapable of change after reaching full development. We now know this is not the case. In fact, the brain is surprisingly malleable.

For instance, many people seem to believe that at age forty, they're too old to change their career, pursue their dreams or acquire new skills. That's simply not the case. Feeling old is mostly a state of mind. You would not believe what some people do in their seventies, eighties or even nineties. For instance:

- Fauna Singh ran a marathon at over 100 years old.
- Anna Mary Robertson "Grandma" Moses didn't start painting until she was 76. In 2006, one of her paintings sold for $1.2 million.
- Nola Ochs, Model Richardson and Leo Plass earned their college degrees at 95, 90, and 99, respectively. Nola started writing her first book, *Nola Remembers*, when she was 100.
- Helen Klein began running when she was 50. Klein wound up running more than 60 marathons and 140 ultra-marathons.
- Julia Child wrote her first cookbook at 50 and went on to become a celebrity chef.
- Colonel Sanders was 62 when he franchised Kentucky Fried Chicken in 1952.

The point is: your brain is more adaptable than you realize. You can choose to create new neural connections at any time, regardless of your age. And as you do so, you are physically rewiring your brain.

My mother is only sixty-two, yet she talks as if she was too old to pursue her dreams or passion projects. Every time she tells me she would have loved doing X, Y or Z, I tell her, "Well, why not start now?" Her answer is always, "It's too late". However, in France, life expectancy for women is over eighty-two years. This being the case, she may have twenty years or more to live. This is a decent amount of time to achieve some serious goals.

Aging might be inevitable, but let's not speed up the process by perceiving ourselves as old. When we choose to use our brain to the best of its abilities, it is a powerful machine, capable of wonderful things. Regardless of age, you can still learn new skills. So, give yourself permission to do so.

* * *

Action guide

You're not too old to reach your goals. In your action guide, write down one thing you've always wanted to do but gave up on because you considered yourself too old (or for other reasons).

Knowing that your brain is malleable and adaptable to change, what could you do to make progress toward that goal?

D. Adopt empowering beliefs about learning

The way you talk to yourself has a major impact on the actions you take and the results you obtain. You cannot act radically differently from what you believe about yourself and about the world. For instance:

- If you believe you're too old to learn a foreign language, what are the chances you'll do so?
- If you believe you're not competent enough to start your own business, what are the odds you'll take the first step in that direction?
- If you believe you're a poor learner, what's the likelihood you'll keep pushing through when you encounter challenges along the way?

Now, when it comes to learning, there are a few empowering beliefs that will have a positive impact on your ability to learn more effectively. In this section, we will review them.

Empowering belief #1: I can always learn and grow. Your capacities aren't fixed. You can always improve and inevitably will—providing you stay consistent with your learning. Every day, you should remind yourself of your ability to learn. Regularly repeat the following affirmation:

"I can always learn and grow."

Empowering belief #2: I can figure things out. As human beings, we are natural problem solvers. The fact we are still here today is a testimonial of that very ability. Consequently, believe you can work things out. You can find a way to learn whatever you need to learn to reach your goals. All the information you need is out there, and you possess the internal resourcefulness to make the most of it. Repeat to yourself:

"I can figure things out."

Empowering belief #3: Learning is an inevitable process. When you stick to an effective learning process, you will learn what you need to learn. Believing that learning is an inevitable process is vital because it will enable you to keep going when you face temporary setbacks and reach inevitable plateaus. Repeat to yourself:

"Learning is inevitable."

Empowering belief #4: I can learn anything faster than almost anybody else. Here is a bonus belief for you:

"I can learn anything faster than almost anybody else."

When you believe you're an incredible learner who can learn anything you desire quickly and effectively, it gives you the boost of motivation you need to acquire knowledge and skills that matter to you. Sure, it may not sound true to you now, but as you start seeing yourself as a fast learner, over time, it will start becoming your reality.

Remember, you can learn anything faster than almost anybody else.

The bottom line is, you're a few beliefs away from transforming your life and radically improving your learning abilities. This is as true for you as for anybody else. Therefore, keep repeating the following statements until they become your reality:

- "I can always learn and grow."
- "I can figure things out."
- "Learning is an inevitable process."
- "I can learn anything faster than almost anybody else."

Action step

Using your action guide, complete the following statements and start building your new identity:

- I can always learn and grow because ...
- I can figure things out because ...
- Learning is an inevitable process because ...
- I can learn faster than almost anybody else because ...

E. Master the learning process

Learning isn't a linear process. It doesn't happen smoothly and easily. To become an excellent learner, you must understand how the learning process actually works. Once you have a more realistic view of the process, you'll be able to keep going and learn whatever you desire.

In this section, I'll explain the different stages of learning—according to my own experience. We'll also discuss the importance of maintaining a positive emotional state during the learning process.

Let's get started, shall we?

Understanding the learning cycle

As we learn, we tend to go through distinctive phases. This learning cycle is made of peaks and valleys, which may be emotionally challenging. It's no wonder many people give up at some point or another. I believe we can identify the following three learning phases:

- **Phase 1: Initial excitement.** Everything is new and you're making fast progress. For instance, you're learning a foreign language and can pronounce a few sentences. You feel good about yourself and are eager to learn even more. You may even imagine yourself becoming fluent in little to no time.
- **Phase 2: First roadblock.** After having made what seems like rapid progress, you now feel as though your progress has slowed. You start doubting yourself. You begin to realize that you had unrealistic expectations. Becoming fluent might take considerably longer than you first thought. In addition, the initial excitement has worn off. Your motivation is low, and you feel like giving up and moving toward something else that looks more exciting. You may also become a victim of negative self-talk. "Why can't I learn faster? What's wrong with me? Perhaps I'm just not good enough." As the results aren't aligned with your expectations, self-doubt creeps in and you consider giving up.
- **Phase 3: Breakthrough.** As you keep going, despite the self-doubt and slow progress, you reach a breakthrough. Suddenly, you feel as though you have made tremendous progress. You feel good and your motivation increases. As a result, you keep learning and return to Phase 1.

The bottom line is this: once you stay consistent with your practice regardless of the way you feel from day to day, you will eventually achieve a breakthrough. In time, you will become an expert.

When learning, the key is consistency and emotional mastery. That is, to learn anything, you must be able to practice regularly and over a long period of time with the inner confidence and knowledge that you will eventually excel at what you do. In that regard, the four beliefs we discussed previously will come in handy. When you develop the core belief that you can always grow and learn, that you can figure things out, that learning is inevitable and that you can learn anything faster than anybody else, you will find yourself in the right mindset to act accordingly and learn effectively. As you do so, learning becomes inevitable.

Practical tips to master the learning cycle

Let's go over some more practical tips to help you master the learning cycle:

- **Celebrate your wins.** You can focus on what you don't know or can't do, or you can focus on all the new things you have learned and couldn't do before. Practice acknowledging the small wins. For instance, if you're learning a new language, notice when you understand a new word, pick up a couple of sentences from a conversation or make complex sentences you couldn't construct before. Then, get excited by knowing that any new thing you learn inevitably moves you closer to your end goal.
- **Visualize the outcome.** Whenever you hit a roadblock or feel like you're not going anywhere, visualize yourself in a few months or a few years when you have reached your learning goals.
- **Focus on the process.** As you visualize yourself having attained your goals, remember that it is by focusing on the process consistently that you will succeed.
- **Accept the way you feel.** When you feel unmotivated, disappointed or frustrated, be okay with that. Don't deny the way you feel. Understand that it's part of the process. In fact, it's a positive sign that you're making progress, reaching new stages in the learning cycle.
- **Remember you can always improve.** Then, remind yourself that no matter how stuck you may feel at the time, you can always improve. If you practice diligently, you'll keep making progress even when it doesn't seem like it.
- **Assume that learning is inevitable.** Whatever you're going

through, remember that learning happens almost automatically when you do the right things. Other people have already learned what you want to learn—and so can you. Release the self-doubt. Yes, it may take you more time or effort to learn than others did, but so what? You'll eventually learn it too.

- **See roadblocks as positive signs.** The simple fact that you have hit a roadblock means that you're moving forward. It's a positive sign you're on the right track, for you cannot hit a roadblock by standing still. Therefore, reframe your thinking and start becoming excited at the idea of the new breakthrough waiting for you.
- **See yourself as someone who perseveres.** Keep telling yourself that you're one of the most perseverant people you know. Giving up isn't something you do. Giving up is just not part of the identity you want to embody and project to the world.

The point is, see yourself as the type of person who can learn anything they desire. Whatever knowledge or skill you wish to acquire, the only unknown is how long it's going to take you. Fortunately, the more things you learn, the better and faster you'll become at learning.

* * *

Action step

Using your action guide, write down a goal you failed to reach in the past. Then, write down what you would do differently if you were to start all over again (now you know about the learning cycle).

F. Make your subconscious work for you

Your subconscious is constantly working in the background, 24/7. While you can only process a limited amount of information consciously, your subconscious is able to process an outstanding amount of data. In fact, a big part of learning involves transferring skills from your conscious to your subconscious.

Since your subconscious is so powerful, it would be a shame not to use it to accelerate your learning. In this section, I'd like to cover a few specific things you can do to help your subconscious work for you.

Put simply, your conscious mind is the goal setter, and your subconscious mind is the goal getter. Your role is then to set goals consciously and communicate them to your subconscious.

Your subconscious cannot differentiate what is true from what isn't. It merely responds to your instructions and acts according to the beliefs you've adopted consciously or, more often, unconsciously. That's why, when internalized at a deeper level, beliefs and affirmations such as, "I can always learn", "I can figure things out", "learning is an inevitable process", and "I can learn anything faster than almost anybody else", will help you become a better learner (i.e., your subconscious will act according to your beliefs).

Now, to boost your ability to learn, you must develop the habit of setting clear goals. Once you have a clear direction, your subconscious will work 24/7, looking for useful information, processing ideas and coming up with ways to make those goals a reality.

For instance, when it comes to book writing, I set yearly goals and continually entertain potential ideas for books I might write months or even years down the road. It doesn't mean I will necessarily write all of them, but I tell my subconscious to be on the lookout and to start:

- Reflecting on potential outlines
- Looking for relevant information, and
- Gathering interesting insights

In other words, I give my subconscious an opportunity to do some work for me before actively starting a book project. Bear in mind that our subconscious does an incredible amount of work in the background whether it is growing our hair and nails, regulating our heart rate or digesting the food we eat. We might as well ask it to help us achieve our goals too, right?

Let me give you a few practical tips you can use to ensure your subconscious works for you:

- **Think of your goals often.** In many ways, you become what you think about most of the time. When you keep thinking of your goal or vision, you begin to make it part of your identity. It becomes your focal point, and the more you think about it, the more you tell your subconscious this goal is critical. As a result, it will look for all the possible ways to help you reach it.
- **Be genuinely excited about your goals.** As humans, we aren't rational. For the most part, we are emotional beings that rationalize our decisions afterward. Our emotions are a powerful motivator. When you can't stop thinking about a goal, when that goal gives you goosebumps, you will often not stop until you attain it. Therefore, get excited about your vision. Which leads us to our next point.
- **Have an unrealistic vision.** Realism is boring. Nobody wants to achieve realistic goals. While having realistic targets for short-term goals is useful, it is not for long-term ones. The problem with "realistic" goals is that they have little energy attached to them. They don't pull you out of bed in the morning. They don't stir your soul and demand you use your talents and gifts. On the other hand, "unrealistic" goals pull you toward the person you wish to become. They demand you develop new skills, cultivate grit and face some of your deepest fears. And, because they are what you truly want, they energize you like nothing else can. Finally, because they may currently seem out of your reach, they require help from your subconscious.
- **Make a commitment to reach your goals.** The most successful people on this planet are committed. Other

people daydream, hope or wish they will reach their goals one day if the stars align. Here is the difference between committing and daydreaming—and it's not a small one. Committing is deciding what you're going to do. It comes with a powerful sense of confidence that what you envision will become a reality. Daydreaming is nothing more than wishful thinking. Daydreaming is when no commitment has been made (yet). Daydreaming is hoping, not deciding. Once you commit to attaining your goals, your subconscious will do whatever it can to assist you. When you daydream, your subconscious will not even consider your request.

- **Create a specific plan to reach your goals.** Writing down your goals using pen and paper is the best way to organize your ideas and clarify your thinking. It seems that the simple fact of writing things down sends a strong signal to your subconscious that these goals matter to you. Few people create written goals, but those who do—and stick to them—often achieve far better results.
- **Visualize your goals.** Visualization is a powerful tool that can help you achieve your most ambitious goals. Practice visualizing your goals every day. How do you feel about speaking fluently in that new language you're learning? How does it feel to play your favorite song on the guitar? The most successful people on this planet use visualization consciously, focusing on what they want all the time. Meanwhile, other people fall prey to their own visualization. They continuously look at how far away they are from their goal and keep worrying about the worst that could happen. Therefore, keep visualizing what you want and feed yourself with the energy of excitement that it produces in you.

* * *

Action step

Using your action guide, write down how you will make your subconscious work for you.

Main takeaways:

1. **Shift your identity.** You can choose to change the way you see yourself at any given time. Choose to perceive yourself as a highly effective learner who can learn anything you desire.

2. **Adopt a growth mindset.** Understand that you can become better and act accordingly. Embrace challenges, persist in the face of obstacles, see effort as a path to mastery, accept constructive criticism and learn from the success of others. Your capacities aren't fixed, so develop a growth mindset to achieve your learning goals.

3. **Understand the power of neuroplasticity.** Your brain is more malleable and adaptable than you think. You can create new neural connections at any time. As you do so, you'll rewire your brain. Regardless of your age, you can still learn new things. So, give yourself permission to do so.

4. **Adopt new empowering beliefs about learning.** What you believe about yourself has a major impact on your ability to learn. Make the following beliefs part of your identity:

- "I can always grow."
- "I can figure things out."
- "Learning is an inevitable process."
- "I can learn almost anything faster than anybody else."

This will make you a much more effective learner.

5. **Master the learning process.** Learning is a chaotic process made of peaks and valleys. Understand that you'll often have to go through different stages before you can reach mastery. First, you'll be excited about learning and will make noticeable progress. Then, you'll

encounter your first roadblock and will become discouraged. Finally, as you stay consistent and keep going, you'll reach a breakthrough. The key is to stay consistent and accept both the ups and downs as part of the learning process.

6. Make your subconscious work for you. Your subconscious is an incredibly powerful machine that works tirelessly, 24/7. Gain clarity regarding your goals and give instructions to your subconscious. The more your subconscious knows where you want to go, the more it will assist you by scanning your environment for useful information or by coming up with creative ways to reach your goals.

7

WHAT SHOULD YOU LEARN?

So far, we have discussed the main misconceptions around learning, discussed what learning actually is, identified common issues and have explained how to develop a learning mindset. Now, it's important we answer two simple yet critical questions together:

What should you learn? And why?

Time is one of the scarcest resources we have. Whenever you dedicate time to a certain activity, you are saying no to everything else you could be doing during that time. The same goes for learning.

For instance, becoming fluent in a foreign language takes thousands of hours of practice. Back when I was a student, I spent well over ten thousand hours learning Japanese. I could have done a lot of other things with all those hours, but I don't regret a moment.

In this section, I would like to discuss the main criteria to consider whenever you want to learn a new skill or acquire more knowledge in a particular area. Too often, we try to learn things for the wrong reasons. As a result, our learning is ineffective and we end up jumping from one thing to the next, never really getting the results we hoped for.

A. The main criteria to consider before learning anything

Now let's go over the key criteria you should consider before picking up any new skills or hobbies. Bear in mind that my list of criteria may not be complete. If you feel as though something is missing, add it to the list. Below are three criteria to consider:

1. **Level of interest.** Do you genuinely *want* to learn that skill? Are you passionate about it? At an intuitive level, do you feel as though it's the right thing for you?
2. **Usefulness.** Will learning that skill help you reach exciting goals? Is it the most effective way to achieve them? Does it move you closer to the person you wish to become? Does it require you to develop self-discipline, confidence, leadership or any other useful traits or characteristics?
3. **Timeliness.** Is right now the best time for you to learn that skill or acquire that knowledge? Is it the highest priority for you or should you learn other more important skills first?

Let's discuss each point in more detail.

1. Level of interest

Learning is far easier—and far more effective—when you have a genuine desire to learn. Having an interest in what you learn is one of the best ways to ensure you'll make progress and acquire the skills or knowledge you desire.

We can divide your level of interest into the following components:

* Interest
* Passion, and
* Intuition

Let's elaborate on each of these components.

Interest. People seldom become excellent at skills they have no particular interest in. Sure, through sheer willpower and strong self-discipline, they might be able to learn somewhat effectively, but it won't be pleasant, and probably not nearly as effective as if they had a strong interest in the first place. Whenever you attempt to learn something new, a strong interest or at least some sense of curiosity is ideal.

Passion. When discussing learning, often not enough importance is given to passion. Yet, passion is one of the most effective learning tools there is. In fact, passion can make up for highly ineffective learning methods. If you are passionate about your subject, you could ignore almost all the learning methods mentioned in **Part III. Watering Your Tree,** or use them inconsistently, and still learn more than most people. More specifically, having a passion for a topic provides you with the following benefits:

- **Incredible energy.** When you do something you love, it doesn't feel like work or study. You love the process and want to keep studying more and more. Sure, you're excited about the results, but you're also able to enjoy the process of learning.
- **Unparalleled grit.** You generally don't abandon something you love—you never quit on your passion. Oftentimes, grit is nothing more than the natural consequence of doing something you're passionate about. As Steve Jobs rightly said, "Often, the people who are successful loved what they did so they could persevere when things got really tough. The ones that didn't love it quit—because they're sane." Yes, there are ways to develop grit, but the question to ask yourself isn't "How can I develop more grit?", but "How can I focus more of my time on the exciting things I will not give up on?"
- **Insatiable curiosity.** When you're passionate about something, you want to learn as much as you can about it, don't you? For you, studying or practicing isn't a chore—it is the inevitable consequence of your need to satisfy your curiosity.
- **Patience.** When you enjoy the journey, you aren't in such a rush to reach your destination. The journey is more

important. So, you keep going at your own pace, overcoming obstacles as they appear.

Intuition. You don't have to learn everything that "makes sense" or seems logical. If anything, we are emotional beings who rationalize our decisions. The point is, just because something is "rational" doesn't mean you should do it. Similarly, just because learning a certain skill or acquiring knowledge in a specific field *seems* to be the smartest thing to do doesn't mean you *should* do it.

For instance, just because you received a job offer with a higher salary doesn't necessarily mean you should take it. Alternatively, just because programming is one of the most valuable skills on the market doesn't mean you should learn it. Many other skills might suit you better and give you a solid edge.

When you try to acquire skills that you have no interest in, the problem is that you'll likely never excel at them. People who love what they do and are naturally good at it will beat you every time. Remember, passionate people have boundless energy, an insatiable desire to learn and will *not* give up. However, if you're learning the wrong skill, it is easier to give up and fail.

Also, beware of well-intentioned friends giving you advice. You don't have to do what everyone else is doing. Sure, they can give you rational advice that makes perfect sense—but they are *not* you. They don't feel the way you feel. They aren't necessarily as passionate about the same things as you.

For instance, when I was building my career as a full-time writer, I received a lot of advice from family and friends. I was told I should do more coaching, sell high-ticket products, create a podcast, organize seminars or be interviewed on podcasts. Yet, I believe the main reason I've been so successful (in my own definition), is that I ignored almost all of them. It wasn't necessarily bad advice—but it was definitely the wrong advice for me *at the time*.

The point is, seek advice and listen to others, but always make the final decision for yourself. Don't try to focus on making "rational" decisions but try to make decisions that speak to you and energize you. Often, we don't do things because they are rational, we do things because we're excited about them.

2. Usefulness

Whenever you learn something new, you should also ask yourself whether it is useful. Remember, everything you do has an opportunity cost—it prevents you from doing something else that might be more useful.

When thinking about the usefulness of a skill, consider the following points:

The level of alignment with your overall vision. Learning can be seen as a way to close the gap between where you are and where you aspire to be. As such, whenever you try to acquire a new skill, ask yourself how that skill will help you move closer to your vision.

Upsides. To be useful, a skill must offer you valuable upsides and, if possible, better upsides than anything else you could be doing instead. These upsides may be career-related or personal-growth-related.

The reach of that skill or knowledge. Ideally, the skills you develop should enable you to acquire ever more useful skills. That is, where possible, you should focus on learning meta-skills that will boost your overall effectiveness and open the door to more effective learning in the future.

Let's look at each of the above points in greater detail.

Level of alignment

The most effective way to design your ideal life is to:

1. Define a clear idea of what you want
2. Identify skills you need to develop to help you get it, and
3. Acquire these skills using effective learning techniques

Now, you may not have a clear vision and may not know exactly where you want to be in five or ten years, but that's okay. Clarity isn't something you get once and are done with it. Clarity is something you refine over time as you gain experience.

For now, try picturing what you want your life to look like in five years. Below are some questions that may help you define your vision:

- What do I *really, really* want?
- If I could learn anything I want and develop any skills I desire, what goals would I pursue?
- What have I always wanted to learn?
- If I were already my ideal self, what skills would I possess? What knowledge would I have already acquired?

Upsides

The reason you learn any skill is that you believe it will benefit you in some way. Therefore, when considering which skill(s) to acquire, identify the main benefits they will provide you. Roughly speaking, we can differentiate between the following benefits:

- **Career-related benefits.** Learning new skills is one of the best ways to accelerate your career.
- **Personal-growth-related benefits.** Learning skills is also a way to improve your personal satisfaction and build your character.

Career-related benefits

Let's face it, some skills are more valuable than others in business. Therefore, when learning a new skill, you must determine whether it is beneficial to you and to your career goals. For instance, below are a few skills that seem to be in demand currently:

Hard skills

- Software development

- User experience design
- Project management
- Machine learning
- Cloud computing, and
- Video and audio editing

Soft skills

- Adaptability and resilience
- Empathy
- Leadership, and
- Communicating and listening

Keep in mind that just because these skills are in high demand doesn't mean you should learn any of them. Based on your career and life goals, the skills you need to learn may be completely different.

Personal benefits

The value of a skill isn't just in what it allows you to achieve, but also —and perhaps more importantly—in the person you will become during and after learning it. When learning, think of the kind of person you wish to become. Then, identify specific skills that could help you build your character and turn into that person. For instance:

- Learning to deliver speeches in front of an audience may boost your self-confidence.
- Training to run a marathon may increase your mental toughness and discipline.
- Practicing meditation every day may increase your patience and sense of well-being.

In short, think of skills both in terms of how they will advance your career goals and build your character. Then, select the skills that will be the most useful in that regard.

Reach of that skill or knowledge

A skill doesn't exist in a vacuum, independent of everything else. When you acquire a new skill, it inevitably opens the doors to new experiences. For instance:

- It boosts your confidence so that you feel more energized, ready to learn more skills (if you were able to learn one specific skill, what else are you capable of learning?)
- It unlocks new abilities, in turn, opening a sea of possibilities for you (when you master basic calculus, you can then learn more advanced math)
- It helps you learn similar skills more quickly (once you learn to speak a foreign language fluently, learning a second language becomes easier)

By 'reach' here, I mean the overall impact the skill will have on your life once you learn it (or as you're learning it). The truth is that some skills are far more impactful than others (i.e., they have a wider reach). What those specific skills are for you right now will, of course, depend on your current skillset and your chosen goals.

More specifically, here is what I mean by 'reach':

Build momentum. Any skill that can help you boost your motivation is good. This is because the more motivated you are to learn, the better and faster you will learn. And the more you learn, the more you'll want to *keep* learning. For instance, perhaps you're learning Spanish and managed to say a few words in Spanish to a native speaker. This makes you feel good, inspiring you to learn more Spanish (and potentially other skills).

Boost your confidence. Any skill that moves you beyond your comfort zone can dramatically shatter your current "model of reality". That is, it can redefine what you think is possible, significantly expanding your field of possibilities. For example, let's say you're shy but summon up the courage to join a public speaking community, like Toastmasters, and deliver your icebreaker (your first speech). Because you originally thought that public speaking was impossible for you, just doing it starts reshaping your sense of identity. You're now wondering what more you can achieve (spoiler: a lot more).

Widen your options. Any skill that gives you more options in life can be said to have a wide reach. For instance, "just" becoming fluent in English dramatically enhances your options. Fluency in English will give you access both to an immense job market as well as a vast amount of information (there are more resources available in English than in any other language). Personally, learning to speak and write in English has been by far the best investment I've made. And you wouldn't be reading this book if I couldn't write in English.

I hope that you now have a solid understanding of what the reach of a skill means.

What about you? If you were to acquire one skill, which one would have the most reach?

3. Timeliness

A skill can be very useful, but the timing may not be right for you. When it comes to identifying the best skills to learn, you must also consider timeliness, which includes thinking about the following things:

What's already on your plate? There is only so much we can learn at any given time. If you're already learning a few skills, consider whether adding one more is realistic.

How much time and energy do you have? Learning takes time and effort. There's no way around it. Do you have enough time and energy to put it into developing that new skill? If you have limited time and energy at your disposal, one trick is to spend only a little time every day on it. It could be ten to fifteen minutes, for example.

How relevant is this skill to you right now? Before learning any new skill make sure you consider how relevant that skill is to you *right now*. Why? Because we forget a lot of what we learn. Consequently, you should use what you learn right away whenever possible. The more you do so, the better it will stick over the long term.

Main takeaways:

In this section, we reviewed the three main criteria to consider when choosing what to learn. These are:

1. Level of interest
2. Usefulness, and
3. Timeliness

Below is a summary:

1. Level of interest

What you choose to learn should be interesting (to you), which entails taking into consideration the following points:

- **Interest.** It's better to learn things you're interested in. Otherwise, you'll need to rely on sheer willpower and iron self-discipline. If your interest is low, the upsides should be *massive* to make that skill worth focusing on.
- **Passion.** Identifying what you're the most passionate about gives you incredible energy, unparalleled grit, insatiable curiosity and great patience. Whenever possible, learn skills that genuinely excite you.
- **Intuition.** When it comes to learning, avoid focusing on making "rational" decisions. Instead, try to make decisions that speak to you and energize you. As human beings, we often don't do things because we are rational, we do things because we're excited about them.

2. Usefulness

What you choose to learn must be truly useful, which entails considering the following things:

- **The level of alignment with your vision.** Learning is largely about acquiring the skills you need to close the gap between where you are and where you want to be. The clearer your vision is, the easier it will be to identify the skills you need to develop to reach that vision.

- **Upsides.** Everything you do comes with an opportunity cost. For a skill to be useful, it must offer major benefits. That is, it must help you reach your career and/or life goals.
- **Reach of the skill/knowledge.** What you learn must be impactful. That is, it must enable you to generate momentum, boost your confidence and/or dramatically increase your options.

3. Timeliness

What you choose to learn should be highly relevant *right now*, which entails respecting the following points:

- **What's already on your plate.** There is only so much you can learn simultaneously. Consider whether adding one more skill is realistic for you, *right now*.
- **Time and energy available.** You only have a limited amount of time and energy. Determine how much time and energy you have available to learn a new skill.
- **Relevancy of the skill to you right now.** We forget most of what we learn, so make sure the skill is relevant to you, *right now*. If you can't put it to use immediately or if it's not a priority, consider learning it later.

B. How many skills should I learn?

Now that we've discussed *how* to decide what you should learn, let's see *how many* skills you should focus on at the same time.

When it comes to achieving learning goals (or any other goals for that matter), focus is *key*. If you have too much on your plate and try to learn too many things, oftentimes, you'll end up giving up on some of the things you're trying to learn. As a rule of thumb, I would advise you to focus on learning no more than three major skills at the same time.

By major skills, I mean things such as:

- Foreign languages
- Disciplines (economy, philosophy, politics, physics)
- Sports activities, or
- Other skills (programming, cooking, public speaking)

How deep should you go with your learning?

How many skills you decide to learn will depend on the level of expertise you want to reach. The better you want to become at something, the more time you'll have to dedicate to learning it.

Below are the two main reasons I recommend focusing on learning only on one or two skills:

1. **You'll make progress faster.** Being focused and remaining consistent over the long term is key to learning anything. The fewer things you're trying to learn simultaneously, the easier it is to do so.
2. **You'll develop transferrable skills.** Learning is a process. The only way to truly understand a skill from beginning to end is to go deep with what you learn. By reaching a high level of proficiency you'll build critical skills such as grit, confidence and enhanced awareness of how the learning process works. As a result, you'll be able to overcome any roadblock, which will serve you well for any subsequent skill you wish to learn.

How much time should you spend learning each day/week?

Now that you have a better idea of the skills you wish to learn, you must decide how much time you'll dedicate to learning them.

There is no clear-cut answer to this, as it will depend on a variety of factors such as how much time and energy you have available each day or how fast you want to learn. However, let me give you some general guidelines. Roughly speaking, we can divide learners into three distinct categories:

- Intermediate learners (3-5 hours/week)
- Advanced learners (5-10 hours/week), and
- Masters (25-35 hours/week)

The main point here is that to learn any major skill that can impact your life significantly, you need to dedicate at least three to five hours of your time to it every week. Anything less than that will likely prove ineffective or will take you too long to acquire it. Think about it this way: if you can't dedicate at least three hours a week to learning a skill, is the skill really that important to you?

The importance of consistency

Once you've decided how much time you'll spend studying each week, you must ensure you stay consistent if you want to see tangible results in the mid-to-long term. Rather than learning something on and off, spend some time learning it each day, or at least three times a week. And do it for months or years.

The key is to start small, and build momentum. Ask yourself: "What's realistic, based on my current situation?" Be on the conservative side. Remember that learning is a marathon, not a sprint. Perhaps you can only spend thirty minutes a day five times a week studying. If so, that's fine. Do that for several weeks until it becomes a habit. Then, once you feel comfortable, ramp up the time you devote to the process.

Effective learners stay consistent in the face of adversity. Consistency acts as their North Star. Meanwhile, ineffective learners rely on motivation, and every setback becomes a reason to give up.

Effective learners (Masters)	Ineffective learners (Dabblers)
Think hard whether to learn a skill	Jump headfirst at the first sign of excitement
Identify clears "why's" behind their goals	Get blindsided by their initial excitement
Set realistic long-term plans	Set unrealistic goals
Rely on consistency to keep them going	Rely on motivation to keep them going
Stay consistent no matter what	Give up when facing roadblocks

The different levels of skills

Not every skill requires months or years of practice before you can learn it. Some skills can be learned in as little as a few hours. Previously, we've discussed major skills, now let's briefly review minor and intermediate skills.

Roughly speaking, we can break down skills as follows:

- Minor skills: 5-50 hours of practice
- Intermediate skills: 50-500 hours of practice, and
- Major skills: 500+ hours of practice

Below is a rough estimate of how many minor/intermediate skills you should focus on at the same time:

- Minor skills: 5-10
- Intermediate skills: 3-5

Let's discuss the main purposes of minor and intermediate skills and how they can fit your overall learning strategy.

Minor skills:

Here are some examples of minor skills:

- Cooking skills (basic)

- Spreadsheet skills (basic)
- Juggling skills (basic), or
- Typewriting skills

Below are the main reasons for learning minor skills.

Stepping stones. Minor skills can act as stepping stones toward some of your main goals. For instance, a certain job or career may require that you polish your spreadsheet skills.

Productivity improvement. Minor skills can increase your overall productivity. For instance, learning basic spreadsheet skills might help you do your work much faster.

Personal enjoyment. You may also learn a minor skill because it's enjoyable or interesting. Perhaps you find it cool to be able to type fast. Or perhaps you're impressed whenever you see someone juggling and want to give it a go.

Desire to belong/ego. We have a strong innate desire both to belong and paradoxically to stand out in some way. For example, you may want to learn how to juggle to impress people occasionally. Or you may want to type fast to differentiate yourself from the "average" person.

When deciding what skills to learn, consider the above points.

Intermediate skills:

Here are some examples of intermediate skills:

- Foreign language (basic conversational level)
- Cooking skills (intermediate level), or
- Disciplines such as philosophy, economics, politics or psychology (basic to intermediate level)

The reasons to learn intermediate skills are fairly like those for learning minor skills. However, they will require more time and effort to develop. Consequently, you must be more selective with what you choose to learn. You can also start with minor skills with the option of delving deeper later.

* * *

Action step

Using the table in your action guide, write down all the skills you're currently learning. Separate them into minor, intermediate and major skills. Then, assess whether you're spending enough time on major skills.

Finally, look at all the things you're learning. Are there any common threads? Are minor and intermediate skills linked to your major skills and overall learning goals or are they disconnected? Are there things you could stop learning or things you want to start learning?

Remember, the more your action and learning are aligned with your goals, the better results you'll obtain in the mid-to-long term.

8
───────

IDENTIFYING YOUR LEARNING GOALS

A. Selecting your learning goals

Now that you have a better idea of what to learn and how much time to dedicate to it every week, let's clarify your learning goals. The more specific you are with your learning goals, the easier it will be to create an effective plan to attain them. Remember this simple truth:

You cannot hit a target you don't set.

Put simply, the point of a goal is to close the gap between where you are and where you want to be. It often entails a shift in your identity. For instance:

- You're a non-Spanish speaker who wants to become a Spanish speaker
- You're an aspiring writer who wants to be a successful writer, or
- You're a non-soccer player who wants to be a competent soccer player

Looking back at everything we have discussed so far, what are the skills you want to learn the most or the knowledge you're the most excited about acquiring?

* * *

Action guide

Using your action guide, brainstorm things that you want to learn in the future. Just write down what comes to mind. For now, don't worry whether you want to start learning them tomorrow or in a decade, and don't even worry whether you'll actually learn them.

Fill in the table below using the action guide:

Things I want to learn	Level of interest (on a scale of 1 to 10	Usefulness (on a scale of 1 to 10)	Relevancy right now (on a scale of 1 to 10)

Now, identify the two or three skills that gathered the most points in the table. These are the skills you should focus on right now. Don't blindly follow this formula though. Ask yourself how you feel about these skills. What is your intuition telling you? Which skill(s) on your list are you the most excited about?

B. Specifying your learning goals

To be truly useful, any goal must help you learn the skills or gain the knowledge you set your mind on obtaining.

By now, you should have identified two to three major skills to focus on. The next step is to set crystal-clear goals. To help you set specific goals, we'll use the following tools:

- Visualizing the result
- Strengthening your "whys"
- Creating the best action plan possible
- Identifying process goals and results goals
- Making your goal SMART, and
- Chunking down your goals

1) Visualizing the result

Before you venture toward any goal, visualize what you want the end result to be like (i.e., what you want the future you to be able to do).

Think of this visualization exercise as a memory. That is, make it vivid and specific. When you tell your best friends about a trip you made to Paris, you don't just tell them it was nice. You explain in detail what you did, what you saw, what you ate, how the weather was and how you felt at the time.

Let's look at a couple of examples.

Learning goal #1—Playing the piano

Imagine that your goal is to play the piano. If so, what would the result look like for *you*? Be specific. Where are you? Who are you with? How do you feel? What are you capable of doing?

For example:

I'm playing a beautiful song on the piano at my brother's birthday. My parents, brothers and sister, cousins and other members of my family are delighted to hear such a beautiful song. They're proud of me. And I'm proud too and feel really good about myself. I'm glad I spent time learning that skill. The time I dedicated to practicing was well worth it.

Learning goal #2—Speaking Spanish

You have decided you want to learn how to speak Spanish. Now, what does the result look like exactly? Where are you? Who are you with? What are you doing? How do you feel about speaking Spanish fluently?

For example:

I'm in Mexico with my Mexican friends. We're having a fun conversation in Spanish while relaxing at the beach. The weather is incredible and the water transparent. I have no difficulties understanding what my friends say, and speaking Spanish is completely easy and natural to me. I'm even cracking a few jokes. All the time I spent studying was well worth it, and I am proud of myself for sticking to my studies.

Do you see how it works? The more detail you can add to the picture, the better. The key is to experience a surge of motivation when you visualize the ideal outcome.

* * *

Action step

Select one skill you'd like to learn. Then, using your action guide, answer the following questions:

- What do you want to learn?
- What do you want to be able to do?
- What level of proficiency do you want to reach?
- What future "memories" do you want your new skill to help you create?

2) Strengthening your "why's"

As the late business philosopher Jim Rohn said, "When the why gets stronger, the how gets easier."

Often, the issue is not so much that we are lazy or lack discipline, it's that we pursue uninspiring goals we care little about. When you're passionate about a learning goal and have dozens of reasons to achieve it, learning becomes significantly easier—if not inevitable.

In this section, we'll look at what you can do to make your goals more enticing.

Find reasons to reach your goal

The more reasons you have to learn something, the more energy you'll have, and the more motivated you'll be to act. Consequently, to be truly effective, you must find powerful whys and make sure they are:

1. **Specific.** Specificity generates clarity and makes your goals much more real. The more clarity you have, the more your subconscious will look for ways to make your goals a reality.
2. **Emotional.** Because something is rational doesn't mean you'll feel inspired to do it. Otherwise, everybody would eat healthily, exercise regularly and refrain from smoking or

drinking alcohol. For your learning to be effective you must "emotionalize" it. The more emotional your why's, the better.

Aligning your learning goals with your values

When what you learn enables you to express your values or create the necessary conditions for their expression, your motivation will be high. Conversely, when you pursue goals that society imposes on you, your motivation will be low.

For instance, some of the things I value the most are:

- **Autonomy:** I want to be able to choose what to work on, where and when.
- **Contribution:** I like to share what I learn, and help others in my own way.
- **Curiosity:** I want to understand better how the world works, which entails traveling, discovering new cultures, learning languages or reading books.
- **Mastery:** I love going deeper with whatever I choose to learn. It provides me with a great sense of satisfaction.
- **Personal growth:** I love learning new things and want to be able to dedicate a lot of time to improve myself.

Whenever I choose to learn something, I do my best to ensure it is aligned with my values.

What about you? What are your values? Is it freedom? Justice? Connection with others? Beauty? Integrity? If you're unsure, take the time to identify some of your core values.

Aim to identify three to five core values.

To find your values, consider the following questions:

- What's most important to me? What things am I unwilling to compromise on?
- When I fail to live by my values, which ones make me feel the most uneasy, misaligned or bad about myself?

- What triggers me? When do I feel as though someone is stepping over my boundaries? In what specific situations does this occur?

You can find a list of values on the website below:

https://jamesclear.com/core-values

Aligning your goals with your interests

Have you ever tried to learn something you're not interested in? If so, you probably struggled, right?

As a rule of thumb, the more excited you are, the better. Remember, people who are the most passionate, learn faster and can persevere for far longer than the average person.

For instance, I love reading books on psychology, personal development or business. It comes easily to me. If anything, I have to stop myself from reading too much. This is why I do what I do. But there are also many things I'm not interested in. For instance, I'm not that keen on cooking, repairing stuff or reading literature. Involving myself with any of these things at a deep level would require tremendous effort and willpower.

The point is, it's far easier to learn things you're genuinely interested in.

Note that it may take a while before you can:

1. Identify clearly what you enjoy doing (self-awareness),
2. Give yourself permission to do it (self-love), and
3. Be okay not learning/doing what others want you to do (self-acceptance).

But that's okay. We are all on the journey toward loving ourselves, embracing our gifts and accepting our shortcomings.

Action step

- Returning to the goal you selected in the previous exercise, in your action guide, write down ten reasons why you *must* absolutely reach that goal.
- Write down the three to five most important core values you aspire to live by

3) Creating the best action plan possible

Many people fail to achieve their learning goals (or any other goals) because they are misaligned with reality. In other words, they aren't doing the right actions to attain their goals—and they fail to notice it. A major problem with this behavior is that it will *never* allow them to grow and learn all the things they want to learn to reach their most exciting goals.

You are the easiest person to fool, which is why you must be *really, really* honest with yourself. Are your actions truly aligned with the vision you want to accomplish?

Now, let me give you an example from my personal life. When I started my blog about personal development, I already had the clear vision that I wanted to have a positive impact on millions of people. I was certainly a bit naïve and didn't realize how hard it would be. However:

- **I knew it could take years, if not decades, and I was prepared for that.** My reasoning was simple: if I keep learning and writing for decades, how can I not become one of the best in the world at what I do?
- **I learned as much as I could about self-publishing.** I read dozens of books, skimmed through countless articles and listened to loads of podcasts on self-publishing. I created thousands of ads on Amazon and spent hours exploring how the algorithm worked. I also looked at the best-sellers in my

category more times than I can count, to get a feel of what a good cover and title looked like.

- **I took massive action and kept writing books consistently.** I wrote and published several books per year to build my brand and increase the odds that one of my books would take off.

By studying everything I could in my field, I was able to identify the most effective blueprint, which entailed:

- Writing books consistently in the same niche (which most successful indie authors do)
- Working on branding and writing books in series (which I took from fiction writers)
- Building an email list of readers
- Understanding the key elements that drive sales (cover, title/subtitle, book description and quality of the content), and
- Learning how to increase the odds that the Amazon algorithm plays in my favor whenever I launch a book

Then, I "simply" followed that blueprint for years until I achieved tangible results.

Note that a blueprint—no matter how detailed and accurate—isn't perfect and never guarantees success, but it will dramatically increase the odds of you reaching your goals. I hope the example above helps you understand the importance of having a sound strategy.

Let's see how you can develop an effective strategy for your own goals, shall we?

How to create an effective learning strategy

Creating an effective learning strategy mainly entails two things:

- Identifying blueprints and best practices, and
- Designing an action plan that works for *you*

Let's go over each of these points in detail.

Identifying blueprints and best practices

By now, you should have clearly defined your learning goals. The next step is to find out the fastest, most effective ways to achieve them. To do so, you should research the best blueprints possible.

Find the best information possible (for you)

To learn as effectively as possible, you must identify the best information. Since you have a specific goal, you can now look for adequate information. Whenever I need to gather information, I like to ask myself the following questions:

- Who has already learned what I'm trying to learn?
- Who knows someone who achieved the same goal?
- Who is most likely to have the information I need (or to know where to find that person)?
- Who is the most renowned expert in that field?

Let's have a brief look at each question.

Who has already learned what I'm trying to learn?

There is no need to reinvent the wheel. If you know someone who has reached a similar goal, try asking them how they did it. In addition, ask them the following questions:

- If you were to learn it all over again, what would you do differently?
- If you were in my shoes, what would you do?
- What's the 80/20 here? That is, what is the twenty percent that would bring me eighty percent of the results?

Who knows someone who achieved the same goal?

If you don't know anybody who reached a similar goal, think of someone who is likely to know someone who did.

Who is the most likely person to have the information I need?

You may not know anyone who has achieved a similar goal, but perhaps you know someone who may have the information or resources you need (or knows someone who does)

Who is the most renowned expert in that field?

Another effective strategy is to identify the most renowned expert(s) in your field. For a few dollars (or even for free), you can receive high-quality information from world-class experts. How? Simply by buying their book or watching their lectures online.

Again, to find the best experts, think of someone you know who could guide you. Otherwise, do your own research online as follows:

Search for the best experts using Google. For instance, you could search "best guitar teacher" or "best marine biologist". Then you can go through the most relevant articles or videos. Once you find a couple of names, I recommend you look on Amazon to see if they have written a book on the subject. Alternatively, you can also see if they have posted some lectures on YouTube and create a dedicated playlist. Finally, another website that can give you good answers is quora.com. Quora is a site where anyone can ask or answer questions.

Word of caution:

When searching online, beware of information overload. Don't try to learn everything and go through every website or watch every video possible. This will lead you to feel overwhelmed. In addition, you will come across contradictory information which will make you doubt yourself and kill your motivation. Therefore, aim at spending no more than one or perhaps two hours researching the best experts. It should be more than enough time.

Below are some general guidelines when researching online. They will help you avoid information overload. For more on how to filter information, refer to the upcoming section, *Overcoming information overload*.

- **Be highly specific with your requests.** Find the best way to put what you're looking for into words. If you type generic words, you'll receive generic answers and you'll spend a lot of time sifting through the information.

- **Select only the most relevant articles or videos** based on their titles and the credibility of the source. For instance, the Harvard Medical School's website is probably more accurate than a random health blog.
- **Click on relevant articles/videos using CTRL + left click** (or command + click if you're on a Mac). This will open a new tab while keeping you on the search page. That way you can open multiple pages in a few clicks and skim through all relevant content in one go rather than going back and forth.
- **Stick to page one of the search results.** If your query is specific enough, in most cases there is little point looking beyond page one of the results. Doing so will probably make you feel overwhelmed without providing you with better information. Only move to page two when necessary, or refine your search.
- **Skim through the articles/videos you've selected.** For articles, skim through quickly. Look at headlines and see if the content is what you're looking for. If not, stop reading and move on to the next article. Rinse and repeat. For videos, check the description to see if there are any timestamps. Then, glance at the comment section to see if someone wrote down a summary of the video. Finally, play the video. You can play in 1.5-2X speed to "skim" the video. If you feel as though it's not what you need, stop watching and move on to the next video.

One thing to realize is that it's okay to discard content as soon as it doesn't seem relevant. Often, we have this fear of missing out. We believe that if we don't read the whole article or watch a complete video, we may miss nuggets of wisdom. Yes, it can happen, but not as often as you think. Therefore, unless you need to do extensive research for a Ph.D., you have nothing to worry about.

By asking people you know for the best resources and using the research techniques above, you'll research more effectively and more quickly while avoiding information overload.

Now, let's look at a concrete example.

Learning philosophy

If you want to learn philosophy, you must first ask yourself what exactly you're trying to learn and why. Philosophy is a vast topic and can be studied for a variety of reasons. Some people might just want to appear smarter. Others might want to use philosophy in a concrete way that will improve their lives (for instance, think of schools of philosophy like Stoicism). Yet others might be interested in improving their thought process and deepening their understanding of the world. The more specific you are, the more you'll know what to look for.

For instance, you could search for "best philosophy book for beginners". As you do so, you can also look at the auto-suggestions to see if there is a query even more relevant to your situation.

Below are some of the results you'll get on the first page of Google:

- 15 of the Best Philosophy Books for Beginners — The apeiron
- 10 Best Philosophy Books For Beginners — Medium
- What are the best philosophy books? — Quora
- 7 Best Philosophy Books for Beginners — Campus Career Club
- The Top 4 Philosophy Books for Beginners (With Synopses)

Now, you can open all the links with the shortcuts above. Then, before you start skimming through all the pages, think of the titles that seem the best to you. Personally, ten or fifteen books sounds like too much to me. First, I would check "The Top 4 Philosophy Books for Beginners". Then, I would have a quick look at Quora ("What are the best philosophy books?"), which tends to offer great answers. However, it can quickly become overwhelming so be careful.

The first link offers the following book recommendations:

- *What Does it All Mean?* by Thomas Nagel, is a brief introduction to philosophy by one of the most influential philosophers of the 20th Century.
- *The Apology* by Plato. A short insight into what Socrates, one of the greatest philosophers, was all about.
- *Famine, Affluence & Morality* by Peter Singer, is a sixteen-page paper discussing ethics.
- *Philosophical Writing* by Aloysius Martinich, is a book explaining how arguments work.

Do any of these books seem interesting to you? Personally, the first book seems like a good place to start. *The Apology* by Plato may be worth giving a try. The third book is a maybe, but the last book doesn't sound that interesting to me at this point.

Let's visit the second link to quora.com. Spending a couple of minutes skimming through the answers, a couple of books stand out to me.

- *Meditations* by Marcus Aurelius.
- *The Story of Philosophy* by Will Durant.

The top Quora answer is actually quite interesting.

"The beginner, in my opinion, should stop after chapter six. That is more than enough for the beginner to ponder. After this overview, the beginner will understand the topic in brief, and will be in a good position to decide what to read next."

So, perhaps I should start with *The Story of Philosophy* and read the first six chapters, before moving on to other resources.

Note that this is merely an example of how to search online for relevant materials.

Identifying the best blueprint

The next step is to identify the best blueprint. Alternatively, you might need to create your own blueprint.

Now, what is a blueprint?

A blueprint is the main strategy to follow to reach your learning goals. It gives you a clear direction and orients most of your actions. Another way to think about it is "strategic learning".

A blueprint can be more or less specific and useful, depending on the nature of your goals. Sometimes, you can copy and paste someone else's strategy. In other situations, you'll have to create your own blueprint and keep refining it over time.

An example of a blueprint is the strategy I used in self-publishing:

I observed successful people in my niche, spent time identifying the strategy they used and "copied" them. However, I then reached a point where I couldn't just rely on that blueprint, and had to create my own. So, I worked on branding and released a book series (among other things).

What about you? What's your blueprint? What's your strategic plan to acquire your desired skills or knowledge?

* * *

Action step

Using the previous goal, reflect on your current blueprint. Is it the best strategy possible? If not, what could you do to find or create a more effective blueprint? Write your answer using your action guide.

4) Identifying process and result goals

We can differentiate between *process* goals and *result* goals. Process goals are the habits you need to implement and the milestones you have to hit to attain your end goals. These end goals are the results goals. In other words, the process goals are the journey, while the result goals are the destination.

Unfortunately, most people obsess over the destination and get discouraged when they fail to see progress. This is the wrong way to think about goals. In truth, a result goal is akin to the destination you program into a GPS. Once you have entered your destination, you don't obsess over it, do you? You let the GPS guide you. Meanwhile, you focus on the road. The same goes for your end goals. The main purpose of a process goal is to help you identify the road to follow. This is why the best way to reach your end goal is always to:

1. Identify the best process to reach your end goal, and
2. Focus all your energy on the process goals

Let me give you one example.

As a writer, I usually have two main result goals for the year:

1. Yearly sales in dollars, and
2. Number of books to sell

Then, my process goals are "simply" to write and publish a certain number of books.

Once I set a destination—book sales in dollars and units—all I need to do is to decide how many books I must write to maximize my chances of attaining my targets. Then, I can create milestones and implement habits to help me hit my writing goal. Of course, this is an oversimplification, but I'm sure you get the idea.

The bottom line is, one of the most important skills you can ever develop is your ability to clarify your learning goals and identify the most effective ways to reach them.

Here is another example of process goals and results goals.

Running a marathon

If your goal is to run a marathon, your process goals and result goals could be as follows:

Process goals:

- Running four times a week for thirty minutes, and
- Doing a long run every ten days

Result goals:

- Running a full-length marathon

Of course, as with the previous example, this is overly simplified. The point is, focusing on the process is the most effective way to reach almost any goal. The key is to stay consistent. Just by writing a few sentences every day, you can have a book in a few months. Just by learning a few words each day, you can learn a couple of thousand words in a foreign language over a year. When it comes to learning, consistency is your ultimate weapon.

Now, let's see how you can make your goals SMART so that you increase the chances of reaching them.

Action step

Look at your previous goal. Then, determine the best process and results goals for it. Write them down in your action guide.

5) Making your goals SMART

Successful people set clear goals that they're determined to achieve. Others engage in wishful thinking and other daydreaming activities. Dreams are not goals. For the most part, dreams can only be achieved once they are turned into crystal-clear goals. As soon as they become goals, they enter the field of possibilities. It's as though you are giving your subconscious the green light to work on them and "manifest" them. To set goals effectively, you can use the SMART goal methodology.

SMART stands for:

- **Specific:** What exactly are you trying to achieve?
- **Measurable:** Can you assess the progress toward your goal easily? How will you know whether you've achieved it?
- **Achievable:** Is it achievable? Is the timeframe realistic? Can you put in the effort required despite all your other responsibilities?
- **Relevant:** Is your vision in line with your values? Does it excite you?
- **Time-bound:** Do you have a clear deadline?

For example, let's say you want to learn Spanish. Your SMART goal could be as follows:

By March 31st, 2022, I will have a fifteen-minute conversation with a Spanish friend in which I will introduce myself and share my future goals.

This goal is:

Specific. You know you must be able to introduce yourself and talk about your goals in Spanish. You'll have to learn enough grammar and vocabulary to be able to do so.

Measurable. While this case may be somewhat subjective, you can still measure your progress by assessing how well your conversation went.

Achievable. Whether your SMART goals are achievable is up to you. You must decide how much time you'll need to spend to reach it, and whether it's realistic for you based on your personal situation. A general rule of thumb is to make it so that you're seventy to eighty percent confident you'll hit your goal. The more experience you have at setting goals, the better you'll become at it.

Relevant. If you love Spanish culture or are passionate about learning languages, this goal can be said to be relevant.

Time-bound. Here you set a clear deadline, March 31st, 2022.

Once you have a clear target to aim at, it becomes easier to hit. You know where to focus and can design an effective strategy to reach your goals.

Most people never achieve their dreams because they fail to put a deadline on them. Don't be like them. Turn your dreams into goals. Then, set deadlines. This is the most effective way to achieve anything you desire.

* * *

Action step

Using your action guide, make your learning goal SMART.

7) Chunking down your goals

As the saying goes, there are no unrealistic goals, only unrealistic timelines. Effective learning entails breaking down your learning goals into small manageable chunks and realistic milestones. Regardless of your goals, they can always be divided into manageable tasks. For instance:

- Instead of reading an entire book, read just one chapter at a time (and practice recalling it).
- Instead of thinking you'll never be fluent in Spanish, just learn a few words and phrases each day.
- Instead of getting overwhelmed at the idea of writing an entire book, write a couple of paragraphs daily.

The point I'm making is that learning is easier when you break down complex topics or advanced skills into their simplest components and set tasks that are manageable for you.

* * *

Action step

What could you do specifically to break your goal down into manageable tasks? Write down your answers in your action guide.

9

IMPLEMENTING YOUR PLAN

Now that you've clarified your learning goals, found role models, identified the best blueprint, and defined process and results goals, it's time to implement your learning plan.

To ensure that you learn as effectively as possible, let's go over the following points:

- Deciding how much time you want to dedicate to your learning,
- Choosing when you'll be studying or practicing,
- Establishing routines, and
- Optimizing your environment.

A. Deciding how much time you want to dedicate to your learning

The first thing you want to do is determine how much time you can dedicate to your learning goal every week. As we've previously seen, you'll have to dedicate at least three hours a week to learn any major skill. For minor skills, it might be less.

Remember, most people try to learn too much too quickly. Feeling overwhelmed, they never develop the consistency required to master anything. So, avoid filling in your calendar with too many things to learn. Keep it simple. Over time, as you acquire more experience, you may try to learn more things.

B. Choosing when you'll be studying or practicing

The next step is to decide when you'll be studying, and to block enough time accordingly. When it comes to getting things done, timeboxing—i.e., blocking time in your calendar for a specific task—is highly effective. For instance, you could decide to spend forty-five minutes studying Spanish each Monday, Wednesday and Friday at 7 pm. Unless you make your learning activities part of your calendar, you won't be consistent, and before you realize it, you'll have dropped whatever you were trying to learn.

Another effective way to stay consistent is to make your learning part of a daily ritual. Morning routines are great for this. You could implement such a routine and decide to read, take online courses or learn a foreign language.

The bottom line is what gets scheduled usually gets done. So, schedule your learning time to the best of your abilities.

C. Establish routines

Everybody gets excited when they start learning something new. However, the initial excitement often doesn't last long. This is why effective learners rely on systems. As James Clear, author of *Atomic Habits*, points out, "You do not rise to the level of your goals, you fall to the level of your systems." The same goes for your learning goals. Therefore, you want to implement routines and build consistency. As you do so, you'll be amazed at how much you can accomplish.

D. Optimizing your environment

With your subconscious picking up information around you 24/7, your environment inevitably plays a part in how productive you are. If you surround yourself with disciplined people who get things done, you'll be compelled to up your game and build more discipline. This is how our mind works.

Having said that, it doesn't mean you should cut off ties with anyone who isn't highly disciplined or positive, but it does mean that, whenever possible, you should surround yourself with people who uplift you and help you upgrade your standards.

Note that it can also be done through books, videos, seminars and so on. For instance, if you only read biographies from the most successful people on earth, you might feel inspired to up your game. The better-quality information you consume, the sharper your mind will tend to become.

Consequently, ask yourself, "Who do I really admire? Who do I want to be like?" Don't just focus on so-called successful people who have made billions of dollars. Really ask yourself, who embodies the values you cherish the most? What kind of people do you truly respect? What are they doing? How are they behaving? What are they thinking?

Your environment is more powerful than your willpower. Perhaps, to paraphrase James Clear, we can say that "you do not rise to the level of your willpower; you fall to the level of your environment." And by environment, I mean:

- Mental environment (the type of information you feed your mind daily)
- Physical environment (the negative/positive incentives that are baked into your physical environment), and
- People environment (the kind of people you're spending the most time with)

When you continuously feed your mind with high-quality information, design an empowering environment conducive to productive work and surround yourself with inspiring people, stepping up your game becomes easy—and learning becomes inevitable.

Action step

In your action guide, write down:

- How much time you can spend on your goal every week realistically
- When you'll be working on the learning goal you've already identified
- One thing you could do to help you stay on track with your learning goals over the long term (i.e., hiring a coach or having an accountability partner)
- One thing you could do to improve your learning environment

So far, we've worked on solidifying the roots to create the proper soil for your learning tree to grow as tall and as strong as possible. We've done this by working on the following components:

- **Awareness:** dispelling myths and understanding what learning is about
- **Mindset:** implementing the proper mindset to learn as effectively as possible
- **Clarity:** prioritizing what you should learn based on several criteria such as level of interest, usefulness and timeliness
- **Strategy:** identifying an effective blueprint and creating an action plan for your learning goals

Now that the roots are in place, it's time for us to work on building a strong tree trunk that will enable you to learn effectively and durably.

PART II

STRENGTHENING YOUR LEARNING TREE TRUNK

One of the biggest mistakes we make when learning is failing to focus enough time and energy on the fundamentals. To maintain the tree analogy, it is failing to strengthen the trunk while adding multiple branches and countless leaves to our tree. Now, you might ask: why is this such a big problem?

It's a problem because it leads us to overload our system with too much irrelevant and unimportant information, and information which is simply too much for us to absorb.

As a result, we will struggle to retain much of what we learn. People often complain that they have a poor memory—and it is certainly true that memory varies from individual to individual. However, the real challenge is usually not a memory issue, it is an *encoding* issue. That is, because they haven't established a solid foundation for their learning (a strong tree trunk), they have nothing on which to attach all the new information they're attempting to acquire.

Let me give you a concrete example. You read a 300-page book on how to learn more effectively. As you do so, you're probably bombarded with the following pieces of information:

- Anecdotes loosely related to the content of the book
- Dozens of tips or advice
- Scientific research on learning
- Stories
- Statistics, and
- Unfamiliar words or concepts

Most of the things I mentioned above can be considered branches or leaves connected to the trunk. If you become too distracted by them and give them more importance than the trunk (key concepts, main points, et cetera), you'll feel overwhelmed, and will retain little from the book.

Yet, this is what we often do. We fail to discriminate between vital pieces of information and less important ones. Remember, as I mentioned when talking about learning misconceptions, not all information is made equal. You must focus on strengthening your tree, not adding more branches, leaves or decorations to it. Otherwise, it will collapse—i.e., you will not retain much from your "learning".

Therefore, a key question to keep in mind always is: what's the trunk here?

- What's the trunk in this article?
- What's the trunk in this chapter?
- What's the trunk in this book?
- What's the trunk in this video?

For instance, what's the trunk in this section? What's the main idea you must remember?

The trunk is this:

When learning, focus on identifying the core concepts and main points and master them.

By doing so, it will enable you to have a solid foundation on which to build more knowledge.

Let's look at what the tree trunk stands for in the framework used for this book in greater depth.

1

WHAT THE TREE TRUNK REPRESENTS

Now, what should our trunk be made of and what should be left out?

Whatever we want to learn, we need to understand the key concepts and grasp the essence of the topic or skills we seek to master. Below are some of the things you should focus on:

1. Core concepts
2. Major principles
3. Laws
4. Theories, and
5. Fundamental moves

Let's look at each of these in greater detail.

A. Core concepts. The understanding of key concepts allows you to create a basis on which you can add further knowledge over time. When you fail to grasp core concepts at a deep level, you saturate your brain, which leads to poor retention and ineffective and/or superficial learning.

For instance, you'll only be able to build a solid knowledge in economics once you understand key concepts like supply and demand, inflation/deflation, monetary policies or the main function of money. You'll also need to define as clearly as possible what economy is at its core. Here is a possible definition:

Economics is a discipline that aims to allocate scarce resources effectively.

If resources weren't scarce, we wouldn't need economics. We would simply get what we want whenever we want, without any trade-offs.

Alternatively, think of politics. If you want to understand politics more deeply, it might be a good idea to make sure you can identify the main characteristics that distinguish right-wing from left-wing policies. You may not agree with this distinction or with the two-party system that exists in many democracies. However, it's a good starting point to help you grasp politics. It gives you a solid trunk on which to build more knowledge and refine your understanding.

The point is, regardless of your learning topics, you must capture the core concepts and increase your understanding of these over time. By doing so, you'll build a solid foundation that enables you to think more accurately and acquire more knowledge over time.

* * *

Action step

Come up with your own definitions of economics and politics. Do not spend more than ten to fifteen minutes to do so. And do not consult a dictionary before you have written down your own definition.

B. Major principles. Principles are mental models that enable you to increase your understanding. They do not reflect reality perfectly (no models ever do), but they are nonetheless useful. The more principles you grasp, the more you can apply them in different situations—and the more knowledge you can acquire.

Below are some examples of principles:

- **The 80/20 Principle.** Twenty percent of what you do generates eighty percent of your results.
- **Neurons that wire together, fire together.** What you keep practicing becomes easier as you create new neural connections or strengthen existing ones.
- **Show me the incentive, I'll show you the result** (Charlie Munger's 'believed' mode). People's behaviors are highly influenced by the incentives they are given or those that are imposed. For instance, in *An Inquiry into the Nature and Causes of the Wealth of Nations*, written almost 250 years ago, Adam Smith explained that "Workmen ... when they are literally paid by the piece, are very apt to overwork themselves, and to ruin their health and constitution in a few years." This is an example of an incentive that is counterproductive.

The more mental models you have in your toolbox, the better decisions you'll make, and the more effective your learning will tend to be. The smartest people on this planet have hundreds or thousands of models to choose from whenever they are making a decision.

C. Laws (Physics). In the stricter sense, laws are mathematical statements. They must be accurate every time or they wouldn't be laws. That is, when we do X, we must get Y every time. A good example is the law of gravity. An apple will fall from a tree to the ground every time. There are no exceptions to this rule. We never see the opposite happening.

Mastering fundamental laws is essential in disciplines like mathematics or physics.

D. Theories

Where laws are based on facts and explain how some part of the natural world works, theories are hypotheses based on rigorous studies and interpretation. Laws never change while theories may evolve over time with new discoveries.

Some examples of theories are:

- The Big Bang theory
- Darwin's theory of evolution
- Einstein's theory of general relativity, or
- Quantum field theory

Mastering key theories in your field of interest is essential to becoming more knowledgeable.

E. Fundamental moves

Fundamental moves refer to the most important moves and techniques that you must master when learning practical skills.

One way we know for sure that fundamentals are key is by looking at what professionals do. When you look at world-class athletes, chess players or actors, you'll notice they continuously return to the fundamentals. They ensure their trunk is rock-solid. Think of martial art experts. They keep practicing the same punches or kicks thousands upon thousands of times.

To sum up, one of the main reasons your learning is ineffective is because you do not spend enough time and effort on strengthening your tree trunk—and you waste too much energy on adding fragile branches and leaves that are ready to fall. With a weak trunk, you have no solid foundations on which to build additional knowledge.

Accordingly, master the core concepts, major principles, laws, theories or fundamental moves required to excel at what you do. Never assume you know everything. If you're not at the top (yet), chances are that you need to go back to the fundamentals and keep strengthening your foundations.

PART III

WATERING YOUR TREE

Now that we've seen what your tree trunk represents, let's discuss what you can do to make it stronger. The stronger your foundations, the better you'll be able to grow your tree of knowledge.

In this section, I'll share with you some of the most effective learning techniques and show you in detail how to make them part of your learning toolbox. Think of these techniques as watering your tree to allow it to grow stronger.

1

THE POWER OF ACTIVE RECALL

 Memory is the diary that we all carry about with us.

— OSCAR WILDE, POET AND PLAYWRIGHT.

Being highly efficient, your mind is reluctant to use more effort than is needed. By exerting effort to retrieve information using active recall, you tell your brain that what you're learning is worth remembering. Retrieval has been shown to be one of the most effective ways to learn. Even when you fail to retrieve what you previously learned, the mere fact you tried will help you learn and retain it.

Active recall is largely underused for many reasons we've already mentioned (misconceptions, lack of understanding of how learning works or simply the lack of willingness to make the effort). In this section, we'll discuss in detail how you can use active recall to learn more effectively. Let's get started.

2

EFFECTIVE LEARNING TECHNIQUES

Active recall entails making an effort to remember what you learn. To this effect, you can use a variety of techniques. Some will be more useful when you seek to learn abstract things such as philosophy, economics or history. Others will be more effective to learn practical skills such as martial arts, sports or cooking.

For clarity's sake, I divided recall techniques into two main categories:

1. Make the effort, and
2. Make effortful recall

"Make the effort" includes recalling methods that require you to "make an effort" such as immediate recalling, mind mapping or teaching. These methods are based on the following principle: Effective learning requires you to make an effort to recall what you learn.

"Making effortful recall" includes techniques such as spaced repetition, interleaved practice or distributed practice. By using these techniques, you will optimize recalling so that you retain information better. It's centered on two science-based principles:

1. The more effort you put into recalling something, the better you'll retain it, and
2. When you recall what you've learned multiple times at spaced intervals, you'll learn better and remember things for longer.

In short, "Make the effort" is the *what* (recalling), and "Make effortful recall" is the *how* (recalling across time according to specific rules). Combining both will enable you to learn more effectively.

Now, let's see in detail the techniques for each category and how you can use them.

A. Make the effort

To learn effectively, you must make an effort, using recall. Below is a list of techniques you can utilize to do so:

1. Pre-test
2. Pre-study recall
3. Immediate recall
4. Mind mapping
5. Summarizing
6. Note-taking
7. Teaching
8. Elaboration, and
9. Doing

Don't worry if it seems overwhelming, though. You don't need to practice active recall for everything you read, watch or listen to. Instead, focus on practicing active recall for the most important things only. And don't beat yourself up when you don't succeed. This book introduces effective learning methods, but these are guidelines to help you learn better. It's something to aim for in the coming months and years. Remember, you can refer to this book as often as necessary. The goal is to improve little by little—at your own pace.

1. Pre-test (tentative recall)

This is when you test yourself on certain material before you begin to study something new. For instance, think of someone who takes a mock test of the SATs before actively studying for it. This technique forces you to draw on everything you've learned up until now (and can recall). This is an effective way to assess where you stand before designing a study schedule. We'll talk more about this in the section on standardized tests.

2. Pre-study recall (previous lesson(s) recall)

This is when you practice recalling what you've learned previously, before starting a new study session. For instance, it could be reviewing the content of the chapter(s) you studied during the last session, or it could be reviewing a couple of chapters you read previously in a business/self-help book before resuming your reading.

Note that by "reviewing", I do not mean rereading what you previously read, going through sentences you underlined or merely checking your notes. I mean using active recall by:

- Summarizing the main points in your head
- Summarizing what you read—in writing—using your own words
- Creating a mind map indicating the main ideas and how they're connected
- Recording yourself using audio and/or video as you explain the main ideas (as if you were teaching them to someone), or
- Writing down your definition of the key concepts

We'll see how to do these things later in this section.

3. Immediate recall (fresh recall)

This is when you make a deliberate effort to recall what you've just read, listened to or watched. For instance, you can practice recalling at the end of a chapter. If the chapter is too long or the book too complicated, practice recalling at the end of a section or after reading a few paragraphs or a couple of pages. When you do so, make sure you use your own words.

Here are a few questions you can ask yourself when recalling:

- **What's the main point?** Because of our tendencies to get hung up on the detail, we must train ourselves to focus on the core message. Think of it as reprogramming your mind or refocusing your lens.
- **What's worth remembering?** Identify what you care about and want to remember.
- **What's still unclear?** If something isn't clear, recognize it and try to gain an understanding. Nobody will judge you.

You can use this technique right after a lesson. For example, after class, try recalling as much as you can straight from your memory for fifteen to twenty minutes. One way to do this is to look at each slide from the course and try to explain it as though you were teaching it to someone else. Another way is to read your notes, identify the main structure and concepts, and elaborate on them.

4. Mind mapping (dot-connecting recall)

This is when you create a map that connects the main ideas in a hierarchical and coherent way. In a way, a mind map mimics the way our brain works. Like our brain, it works through association. For instance, when you think of the concept of "learning", some words and ideas automatically pop up into your head. Perhaps the following words or ideas came to mind:

- Memory
- Speed reading
- School
- Education
- Machine learning
- Books
- Exams
- Knowledge, or

- Wisdom

This is how your brain works. It associates ideas. Each idea is also associated with even more ideas. It's like a tree with branches divided into more branches.

When you write ideas on a sheet of paper, it forces you to think linearly rather than by association of ideas. It can be effective when you want to sharpen your thinking and increase your understanding of a specific concept. But when you want to recall what you learn in a more structured way, mind maps come in handy.

How to create mind maps

To create a mind map you can simply:

- Take a sheet of paper (or use an app) and write the topic in the middle.
- Create different branches for related ideas or concepts. Often, it can be the different parts or chapters of a book.
- For each idea, add more branches to illustrate sub-ideas.
- Write down specific examples for sub-ideas.

Note that your mind map will be organized in different ways based on the content of your learning. For example, it can be:

- Chronological (historical dates)
- Spatial (continents or countries)
- Describing different parts of a whole (parts of the body or components in a computer), or
- Logical (description of a process or development of an argument)

The material you're consuming will often provide you with an outline you can reuse when practicing recalling information. However, you can also reorganize it if needed. If you need to make a synthesis of several documents, you'll probably need to create your own outline (like when writing an article or a book).

5. Summarizing (filtered recall)

This is when you write down from memory what you learned.

The truth is, you can learn something by heart, but it doesn't mean you understand it. Just because you take notes, copying verbatim what the teacher says, it doesn't mean you understand and can recall the topic.

We all use different words when speaking. Our vocabulary reflects our educational background, centers of interest and political or religious views.

This is why copying what you read, listen to or hear can often be ineffective. Instead, you must translate external thoughts and ideas into words that speak to you, which entails using your own words.

Below are the main benefits of summarizing:

- **Helps identify key points.** To summarize anything, you must be able to identify the main points. This entails asking yourself the following question:
- "What's worth including in the summary, and what should be left out?"
- **Requires you to use your own words.** To summarize, you must use your own words. By doing so, you automatically write in a more memorable way, which makes it easier for you to retain the content.
- **Enhances your learning.** Summarizing forces you to recall what you've just learned. And, as we've seen before, recalling information increases memory retention by signaling to your brain the content is worth memorizing.
- **Exposes any gap in knowledge.** As you explain what you learn, it will become apparent which concepts or ideas you don't understand as well as you thought. You can't come to this realization just by copying what's in your textbook.

6. Note-taking (real-time recall)

Most people do not know how to take proper notes, and in most cases, taking notes might not be useful. For the note-taking process to be useful, it must be aligned with the most effective learning techniques we discuss in this book. The point of taking notes is to enhance your learning, not to go through the motions or feel good about yourself by creating the illusion that you're learning. Below are some ideas on what to do to ensure the notes you take are useful:

- **Have a clear goal.** Try to identify what exactly you hope to gain from taking notes. What specific things do you want to learn? How will you use your notes later? What purpose will they play in your learning program? Are they a way for you to stay engaged during a lecture? Will you use them to add personal comments and opinions on what you hear?
- **Write down what matters to you.** Taking notes must be personal. It's not simply about copying what you hear. Therefore, make sure you paraphrase what you hear using your own words. Make comments. Connect the new information with the ideas you already know. Come up with your own examples.
- **Review your notes.** Go through your notes as soon as possible after your note-taking session. Then, add information you may have forgotten to write (or didn't have time to write). Put in everything you deem relevant for your learning. By doing so, you will practice active recall effectively, which will increase your overall retention.
- **Review your notes as often as necessary.** Don't just read them. Look at the main concepts and try to recall them. Teach them to someone or summarize them, using pen and paper. If necessary, create mind maps or flashcards. As Barbara Oakley wrote in *Learn Like a Pro*, "A study of medical students found that students who made As almost always reviewed the lecture the same day, while C-grade students almost never did so."

Question whether you should take notes

Random note-taking isn't effective. Question whether you should even take notes in the first place. There are many situations where you will be better off creating flashcards, summarizing what you read, teaching the basic concepts to friends or recalling key bullet points. You should probably only take notes in cases where you can't get your hands on any study materials. Fortunately, nowadays, we usually have access to recordings of lectures, PDF summaries or textbooks, which makes taking notes less important.

Take notes after, not during lessons

Another option is to take notes after a lecture or after reading a section of a book. Listening or reading and taking notes at the same time is not ideal.

Taking notes right after class will force you to practice active recall, which will help you retain the material better. Remember, the more effort you exert, the better you will learn. Avoiding taking notes during class will also enable you to listen more carefully, which will increase your comprehension of the topic.

Similarly, if you attempt to take notes while reading a book, you will most likely end up copying verbatim what is written in the book. A much better way to approach learning is to close the book after reading a section, then summarize the content in your own words. Again, this forces you to practice active recall, which will make your learning more effective.

How to take notes during lectures

When taking notes, below are two note-taking methods you might benefit from using.

Split notes

This note-taking method is what Barbara Oakley recommends in her book, *Learn Like a Pro*. It works as follows:

- Draw a vertical line one-third of the way across the page.

- Capture main ideas on the right of the vertical line.
- Then, summarize the main ideas in a few words in the left-hand column. You can do this either during lectures or afterward.
- If possible, review your notes the same day. When you do so, cover the right-hand side and quiz yourself to see how much you can recall.

Capture and create

This note-taking system is what Jim Kwik recommends in his book, *Limitless*, and it works as follows:

- On the left side, you're *taking* notes (capturing).
- On the right side, you're *making* notes (creating). That is, you write down your impression. Ask yourself why the information matters, how you can use it, or what it reminds you of.
- Review your notes immediately after your note-taking session is over.
- Add any information you might have missed while taking the notes.

How to take notes when reading a book

You certainly don't need to take notes all the time, trying to remember every point in every book you read. However, for interesting books, you might want to spend extra time taking notes, so that you can remember them better, or refer to them later.

Let's see what you can specifically do to help you get more out of the books you read.

Set a goal

Before you start reading any book, it's a good idea to have a goal in mind. For instance, if you do research, you won't approach a book the same way as when reading for pleasure. By knowing what you want to get out of a book, you'll be able to make the most of your reading.

Let's say you are trying to find a specific piece of information. In this case, you might go through several books and only read one relevant chapter in one of these books. On the other hand, if you're learning about a more general topic, it might make sense to read a book on that topic from cover to cover. It all depends on your goal.

Skim through the book

Whenever you start reading a book, spend a few minutes skimming through it. This will give you a better sense of what the book is about, which will also help you decide whether you want to read all of it, part of it or none of it. Understanding how the book is structured will also help retain more information.

To skim through a book:

- **Read the title and subtitle carefully.** This is obvious, but worth mentioning. The title and subtitles (for non-fiction books) will generally tell you what the book is about and what it will cover and not cover. This will help you decide whether the book is likely to include the information you need.
- **Review the table of contents.** Read the table of contents and try to understand what the book is about, and how it is structured. How many parts are there? What's the logic? What information seems to be covered? What seems to be left out and why?
- **Read the introduction and conclusion.** Read the introduction and try to identify the main thesis and key arguments. Then, read the conclusion and identify the main lessons and key points covered in the book.
- **Read summaries at the end of each chapter.** Sometimes, the author lists the main takeaways at the end of each chapter. If so, go through them quickly.

Decide what to do with the book

If, after skimming through the book, you notice that it's not what you're looking for, don't feel obligated to read it. If only one chapter piques your interest, then read and recall that chapter. Books are learning tools. Use them to acquire knowledge, but don't become enslaved by them. You are the one dictating the rules, not the book's author.

How to take notes (physical books)

Reading is having a conversation with the author of the book. Marking a book will keep you engaged, and make you think more as you read. Combined with recalling techniques, this is an effective way to learn.

In *How to Read a Book*, Mortimer J. Adler recommends that you mark your book as follows:

- **Underline** major points or important statements.
- **Use vertical lines at the margin** to emphasize a statement you have already underlined or to point to a passage that is too long to be underlined.
- **Draw asterisks in the margin** to stress the ten to twelve key statements or passages in the book.
- **Write numbers in the margin** to indicate a sequence of points that the author makes to develop their argument.
- **Write other pages' numbers in the margin** to mention where else in the book the author makes the same points (or contradictory points). It can also be used to connect ideas that belong together (though they may be separated by many pages).
- **Write in the margin, or at the top or bottom of the page** to note questions that a passage raises in your mind, to summarize a complicated argument or to make relevant comments.

How to take notes (eBooks)

When reading eBooks, you cannot mark the book the same way you can with physical books. However, in most cases, you can do the following:

- Highlight key sentences.
- Write comments.
- Export highlighted sentences and comments.

For instance, I mostly read Kindle eBooks. Every time I read a book, I make sure to highlight the points I find the most important. Then, when I need to refer to a specific book, I can go through the highlighted sentences quickly, knowing I'll get the gist of the information it contains.

Going one step further, I export the highlighted sentences and send them to my email as a PDF file. Later, I create a folder in which I include all the books covering the same topic.

This is a simple system that gives me easy access to the information I need when writing a book.

Create mind maps

You can also use mind maps to summarize the books you read whether using pen and paper or via specific apps, such as *Mindomo*. Some examples are:

- Creating a mind map from memory of a chapter you just finished reading.
- Creating a mind map of an entire book you finished reading.

Remember, the key is to practice active recall. Try to remember as much as you can from a chapter or a whole book without rereading it. Focus on key concepts and how they are interconnected. Then, try to remember specific examples from the book or come up with examples of your own. Ideally, you want to be able to teach the concepts in the articles or books to a friend in a concise and precise manner. With practice, you'll become better at extracting key concepts and internalizing them.

Bonus tip:

When you read a book, tell yourself that you might need to teach it to a specific friend later. This alone will help you be more intentional with your reading and, consequently, you will retain more information.

Use book templates

Another way to remember what you read is to make brief summaries using a book template. For example, the doctor and YouTuber, Ali Abdaal, uses a template containing the following information:

- **The book in three sentences/points.** This is a section in which you summarize the three main points taken from the book. The idea is to use only one sentence per point, but it's fine if you need to write a few sentences.
- **How the book changed me.** In this section, you can write how the book has changed your life, your behavior, your thoughts and/or your ideas. This is a good way to make sure you capture the main practical lessons from the book.
- **My Top Three quotes.** Use this section to write your favorites quotes from the book.
- **Summaries + Notes.** In this section, you can write a summary of the books by chapter. It's up to you how much detail you want to include.

This is but one example of a template. When summarizing, the key is to write down the main concepts that are the most useful and relevant to you, and to think of specific ways to apply them in your life.

7. Teaching (structured recall)

This is when you teach what you learn to someone else. Teaching is one of the most powerful—and underutilized—ways to learn. It presents many benefits, including:

1. **Shedding light on what you don't understand.** To teach something effectively, you must understand it well. Teaching will enable you to identify any gaps in your knowledge.
2. **Forcing you to summarize what you know, and to organize your knowledge.** To teach effectively, you must develop a

curriculum that follows a certain logic. This process will lead you to organize your knowledge and deepen your learning.

3. **Making you think of ways to keep students engaged.** To facilitate learning, you'll have to come up with concrete examples, useful metaphors, interesting analogies, practical exercises and so on. This will reinforce your learning.

4. **Gaining more understanding through interactions with students.** Students will ask you questions, putting your knowledge to the test. The more you interact with students, the more you'll strengthen your understanding of the topic.

While writing this book, I had to refine my understanding of the learning process to come up with an outline that is both effective and easy to understand (points #1 and #2).

Then, every time I made a point, I had to provide you with metaphors, concrete examples or analogies to get it across (point #3).

Finally, though I didn't receive questions directly from you, I interviewed a few of my subscribers and did my best to put myself in the shoes of my readers. I asked questions such as, "Does this structure make sense?", "Is this example relevant?", "Is this exercise useful?" (point #4).

The bottom line is this. Teaching is one of the most effective ways to learn. You cannot properly teach what you do not fully understand. For any important topic you want to master, consider teaching it. Now, it doesn't have to be live, nor do you have to teach it to dozens of people. Below are examples of what you could do:

- **Teach it to a friend or colleague.** For example, next time you meet a friend, teach them what you learned from a book in your field of interest. And let them ask you questions.
- **Create an online course, video or article.** Put together content and publish it online. This will force you to sort out your thoughts, structure your learning and deepen your knowledge.
- **Organize a webinar, conference or presentation.** Make a

presentation on the topic whether at work, online or at your local library.

- **Join or create a book club.** Become part of a book club in which you'll discuss a particular book and share what you learned every week/month.
- **Mentor someone.** When relevant, find someone to mentor. Mentoring is a great way to keep your knowledge up to date and deepen your understanding of a topic.

To sum up, teaching is the ultimate tool, because it combines many effective learning techniques such as:

- **Recall.** You must recall what you learned every time you teach something and when you create the teaching material.
- **Chunking.** You need to structure your learning which is somewhat akin to chunking (breaking down knowledge into easy-to-follow steps).
- **Summarizing.** You need to summarize your learning in your own words to create a curriculum and a presentation.
- **Spaced repetition.** You will be exposed to the topic repeatedly as you create and teach the course.
- **Elaboration.** You must develop concrete examples, analogies, metaphors and other teaching tools to improve the learning experience.

Therefore, if you want to know how much you've learned from reading this book, try to teach its content to one of your friends. You'll instantly discover what you know and what you don't know.

8. Elaboration

This is when you come up with additional examples to illustrate what you're learning.

Building a solid understanding of a discipline isn't easy and requires time. One way to boost your understanding and increase memory retention is to play around with concepts.

Here is what I mean by that:

Recall specific examples given for the concept (from a book you read or video you watched).

When you learn a new concept, try to remember the specific example given to illustrate it. Then, think of that example when you want to explain it to someone. For instance, in this book, I compare learning to growing a tree (roots, trunk and branches/leaves). As an exercise, try to recall what each element of the tree consists of. Below is a brief reminder:

- **Roots:** These are the foundations that enable your tree to grow taller and stronger. That is, understanding what learning is (awareness), developing a powerful learning attitude (mindset), identifying what to learn (clarity), and creating an effective action plan (strategy).
- **Trunk:** This represents the core concepts, key principles and fundamental moves you need to master to learn more effectively and increase retention.
- **Branches and leaves:** These stand for sub-concepts, facts, stories, anecdotes or statistics you can add to expand your fundamental knowledge.
- **Water:** This represents the learning techniques that will strengthen your tree, such as recalling, summarizing or teaching.

For instance, to illustrate the concept of supply and demand in economics, we can give the specific example below:

Supply/demand—Rent in Estonia during COVID. In Estonia where I live, rent declined during the COVID crisis. In absence of tourists, landlords who used to do short-term rentals via Airbnb moved into long-term rentals. More apartments being on the market (increase in supply) for the same number (or fewer) tenants (similar or lower demand), led to a reduction in rent.

* * *

Action step

Come up with specific examples to illustrate a new concept. To go further, create your own examples from your personal life or from the life of people you know. When necessary, make up examples.

Create metaphors/make analogies.

Another way to practice elaboration is to develop metaphors or analogies. Let's say you want to illustrate the concept of "elaboration". We could use the metaphor of a stool. At first, a new concept is akin to an unstable stool. As we find one specific example, it becomes a one-legged stool. At this point, the concept may still be unclear. As we come up with an additional example, now our stool has two legs, showing a better grasp of the concept. If we add a couple more examples, we will end up with a stable stool and the concept will become clear in our minds.

By using metaphors and analogies, we create anchors to which we can attach any new concept. Truth is, we are far better at remembering images than words. As the saying goes, a picture is worth a thousand words.

9. Doing (unconscious recall)

Another effective, yet underused tool to learn effectively is doing. I've met a lot of people who failed to reach their goals because they didn't take enough action, but I have yet to find someone who failed because they took *too much* action. The point is, in many cases, what you need to do is take more action.

By taking action, I mean learning in a real-life situation. I call it having "skin in the game", in reference to the title of Nassim Taleb's book. Having skin in the game means that you put yourself in real-life situations that are somewhat stressful and uncomfortable. Such situations require that you stay hyper-focused, which forces you to learn and grow. The more skin you have in the game, the more your brain is stimulated the right way, and can develop the neural connections needed to learn. Your brain will learn much faster by being exposed to real-life situations.

When I decided to learn Estonian, I hired a teacher online to practice speaking the language. The first sessions were quite stressful. I never felt ready. I had to stretch myself continuously. I could have gone the easy way by using an app on my phone and learning from the comfort of my sofa, but I would likely still be unable to create a proper sentence, let alone understand a basic conversation.

The principle is simple. Put yourself in situations where you're most likely to learn the desired skill. This is common sense, right?

- Want to learn public speaking? Deliver a speech in front of a real audience.
- Want to become a life coach? Find real clients and start coaching them (even if you need to do it for free at first).
- Want to become a writer? Start writing.

Main takeaways

1. **Pre-test.** Test yourself before you start studying for a test or exam to assess where you stand before designing an effective learning schedule.
2. **Pre-study recall.** Practice recalling what you've learned previously before starting a new study session.
3. **Immediate recall.** Make a conscious effort to recall what you just read, listened to or watched. Ask yourself, "What's the main point? What's worth remembering? What's still unclear?"
4. **Mind mapping.** Create a map to connect the main ideas in a hierarchical and coherent way.
5. **Summarizing.** From memory, write down what you learned in your own words. This will help you identify key points and expose any gaps in knowledge, thereby enhancing your learning.
6. **Note-taking.** Before taking notes, ask yourself whether you really need to. If you do, ensure that you have a clear goal,

that you use your own words and that you review your notes afterward.

7. **Teaching.** This is one of the most powerful learning tools, as it combines various components of effective learning. Therefore, teach what you learn to others whether by creating a video, writing an article, delivering a seminar, mentoring someone or merely by sharing the main points with a friend or colleague.

8. **Elaboration.** Whenever you try to acquire a new concept, recall specific examples, create metaphors or make analogies that speak to you. If you can't give examples or metaphors to explain something, you probably don't know the subject well enough.

9. **Doing.** Learn by doing. Put yourself in real-life situations where your brain will be forced to create the neural connections required for learning. Drive a real car, coach real people, speak in front of a real audience and so on.

Now that we've seen how to practice recall, let's see how you can develop your recalling skills even more effectively, using *effortful recall.*

B. Make effortful recall

Forgetting is an important part of learning. By forgetting and recalling, we eventually acquire knowledge that will stick long term. *Effortful recall* is based on the following principle: by trying to recall what we learn on a regular basis, we send a signal to our brain that the information is worth remembering. Also, by giving our brain time to process information between two learning sessions, we enable it to work in the background, thereby improving our ability to learn.

Now, let's see the main techniques you can use to practice effortful recall. These are:

1. **Spaced repetition.** This is practicing active recall multiple times at set intervals.

2. **Distributed learning.** This is spreading your learning to

make consistent progress over time. For the sake of this book, we differentiate distributed learning from spaced repetition since it's also about practicing (i.e., learning something new), rather than being just about recalling things we have previously learned.

3. **Interleaved practice.** This is a technique that entails rotating between various exercises. When done well, this system has been shown to be more effective than practicing the same thing repeatedly.

Let's elaborate on each technique.

1. Spaced repetition

Have you ever crammed a few days before an exam? If so, how long after the exam did you remember the information?

Cramming can be effective when it comes to learning a huge amount of information over a short period of time. However, such learning has been shown to be ineffective in helping you retain information for the long-term. To become a more effective learner, you must replace cramming with spaced repetition. That is, you must space your learning so that it is more regular and more consistent. Doing this has been proven to help students remember more, and for a longer period.

To illustrate the effectiveness of spaced repetition, let's look at a study of thirty-eight surgical residents, as presented in Peter C. Brown's book, *Make it Stick*.

In this study, the surgical residents were asked to take four short lessons in microsurgery. Half took the four lessons in one single day, while the remainder completed the same lessons with a week's interval between them.

When given a test a month later, the second group outperformed the first group significantly in all areas (time to complete the surgery, number of hand movements and success at reattaching the severed, pulsating aortas of live rats.) Even worse, among the residents who completed the four lessons in one day, sixteen percent "damaged the rats' blood vessels beyond repair and were unable to complete their surgeries."

How to practice spaced repetition

You now understand that reviewing what you learn multiple times is one of the best ways to improve your learning, but you may wonder how often you should do so for optimal results. The answer isn't clear and will depend on a variety of factors such as:

- **How long you want to retain the information.** The longer you want to memorize something, the more times you'll need to practice effortful recall. This is why students who cram before exams tend to forget most of what they learned. Meanwhile, people who are passionate about a topic and keep studying it, can remember an astounding number of facts and details for years.
- **How much you already know and how solid your foundations are.** When you start learning a new discipline, you'll likely need to practice recalling more often. As you internalize your learning over time, you will be able to space out your learning sessions a little more. Obviously, the more proficient you want to be, the more you'll have to practice.

General guidelines

While there are no clear-cut answers regarding how often you should use spaced repetition, the following guidelines will help.

One common pattern for spaced repetition is to use the following intervals:

One day, two days, one week, two weeks, then one month.

For instance, let's say you want to remember the important events leading to the fall of the Roman Empire from your history textbook. In this case, you can practice recalling the next day, wait a couple of days, then delay a week, then delay for a couple of weeks, and finally a month before you practice recalling. If you want to remember what you learn for years, you can go one step further and review the material again in a couple of months, then in six months, and in one year.

Emphasize what you *don't* remember

Spaced repetition is even more effective when you give additional weight to the material you struggle to retain. If you can remember the content of a chapter correctly several times in a row, you may not need to review it as often. However, if you keep getting specific answers wrong or can't remember the details of a certain chapter, recalling it more often will help. Perhaps review it every day or every other day until you get it right before spacing the review sessions further apart.

Use flashcards

It's not always easy to design the correct spaced repetition system. This is when flashcard apps can be handy. Many such apps like *Anki* have a built-in spaced repetition system. For instance, *Anki* will show you cards you struggle to remember more often than the ones you recall easily. You can even customize the settings based on your needs. Among other things, you can use flashcards to:

- **Memorize words in a foreign language.** You can write a word in a foreign language on one side of the card and the definition on the other side (or download/purchase such decks).
- **Learn concepts.** You can write the name of a concept on one side of a card and its definition with examples on the other side.
- **Review and prepare classes.** You can also create flashcards to review classes or study for exams. Some medical students rely heavily on flashcards. Doctors and YouTubers, Mike and Matty, have created many videos explaining how to study using flashcards. They have even created a free note-taking tool called *RemNote*. If you're interested in implementing such a system, check their YouTube channel or download their note-taking tool. (same)

When and when not to use spaced repetition

Spaced repetition will be the most useful in the following situations:

- At school
- To prepare for exams (e.g., SAT, GMAT, language proficiency tests, et cetera), or
- For rote learning in general (e.g., learning vocabulary in a foreign language)

Spaced repetition will be less appropriate in the following situations:

- Practical skills (cooking, sports or driving), or
- Anything that requires little or no root memorization

For any skills that require real-life experience and practice in complex settings, the techniques discussed further in this section—interleaved practice and distributed learning—will be more important.

2. Distributed practice

Distributed practice is a learning method that entails spreading out your learning to make consistent progress over time. It is somewhat different from spaced repetition in that it's not just about recalling what you previously learned per se, but it is also about practicing and learning new things. By leaving time between two practice sessions, you give your brain room to create and solidify new neural connections.

A good analogy is to compare the process to physical exercise. When you want to gain muscle, you stress the muscles you're trying to develop by exerting effort. You then need to give them some rest before the next workout session. It would be highly ineffective to spend eight hours a day striving to develop the same muscle. You would just end up hurting yourself. Similarly, cramming all day long for days on end is an ineffective way to retain knowledge over the long term. Instead, you need to space out your practice.

Concrete examples of distributed practice

Let's say you want to study Spanish for five hours a week. In that case, it will be more effective to study one hour a day for five days than to study for five hours in a row every Monday. Studying every weekday will ensure you sleep on what you learned while continuously learning new material each day (and recalling older material). It will also prevent you from forgetting too much. Meanwhile, even though studying once a week may be enough to maintain your current skills or even improve slightly, it will be harder for you to develop your skills consistently.

The point is you want to find the balance between consistency and intensity. Sure, if you have the time to study for hours each day, that's great, but for most people it's unrealistic. Remember, for any meaningful goal, aim at spending at least thirty to forty-five minutes a day practicing or studying. If you can't do that daily, two to three times a week is a minimum.

3. Interleaved practice

In the past, we assumed that working on the same skill, or trying to solve the same type of problem repeatedly, was the best way to learn and improve performance. However, studies show that, while practice and repetition are essential components of learning, this is not the most effective method. Mixing various exercises has been shown as a better way to learn. This is usually referred to as "interleaved practice".

What is interleaved practice and how does it work?

Interleaved practice involves alternating between various exercises within the same category.

For instance, let's say you need to learn the content of three chapters from a textbook today. You may naturally lean toward studying chapter one in the morning, chapter two in the afternoon, and chapter three in the evening. Now, with interleaved practice, you would go over all three chapters in the morning. Then, you'll repeat the same process in the afternoon and in the evening. By doing so, you would have reviewed the same material three times while leaving time for your brain to consolidate the information.

Usual learning method		
Morning	**Afternoon**	**Evening**
Chapter 1	Chapter 2	Chapter 3

Interleaved practice		
Morning	**Afternoon**	**Evening**
Chapter 1	Chapter 1	Chapter 1
Chapter 2	Chapter 2	Chapter 2
Chapter 3	Chapter 3	Chapter 3

If you have three days to study, on the first day you can study chapter one in the morning, chapter two in the early afternoon and chapter three in the late afternoon. Then, you can repeat the same process for the remaining two days.

The following study, described by Peter C. Brown in *Make it Stick*, clearly shows there is some value in mixing your practice and adding variations rather than doing the same thing over and over.

A group of eight-year-olds practiced throwing beanbags into a bucket. Half of the kids tossed them into a bucket three feet away while the remaining half alternated between tossing the beanbags into buckets two feet and four feet away. After twelve weeks of practice, all the kids were asked to throw the beanbags into a bucket placed three feet away. The kids who had practiced on two- and four-foot throws significantly outperformed the other kids. Yet, they never actually practiced throwing into buckets placed three feet away.

The point is, rather than studying one thing before moving to the next, rotate between various things you need to learn. Remember, your brain will need to make effort each time you try to recall what you previously learned. By rotating the topics or the exercises, you will increase the number of active recalls while spacing them across time. In addition, by giving yourself limited time to study one specific thing during a set session, you'll make your brain work harder when recalling later, which will boost retention. These two factors (rotating and effortful recalling) will make your learning much more effective.

We've seen one example of interleaved practice when learning something abstract. Now, let's see examples of interleaved practice for more practical skills.

For instance:

- If you practice tennis serves, you can alternate between different variations (flat serve, slice serve and kick serve).
- If you work on your baseball batting skills, you can vary between fastballs, breaking balls and changeups.
- If you practice basketball three-point shots, you can shoot from various positions outside of the three-point line.

To conclude, the main benefits of using interleaved practice seem to be as follows:

Leverage spaced repetition. Interleaved practice provides a form of spacing, giving time for the brain to develop and strengthen neural connections, which enhances learning and retention.

Strengthen the brain's adaptability. Interleaved practice enhances your ability to discriminate between different kinds of problems. As a result, it trains your brain to be more adaptable when facing real-life situations which are often unpredictable.

Build deeper learning. Thanks to the two benefits above, interleaved practice helps people learn better and at a deeper level. Probably because it makes the brain work harder.

The point is this: your brain learns by exerting effort. Variability and unpredictability—along with the time given to the brain to consolidate the information—seems to optimize brain performance and improve learning. Therefore, make sure you use interleaved practice whenever suitable.

Now that we've seen the most effective learning techniques, let's go over one major issue many learners face: information overload.

PART IV

PRUNING THE TREE

Information overload is one of the biggest issues you'll face when learning. If consuming more information was the solution to achieving any goal, we would all be much more successful than we actually are.

In this section, we'll discuss information overload, as well as Shiny Object Syndrome. We'll see why people often fall prey to these issues, and what you can do specifically to overcome them. To extend our tree metaphor, information overload is akin to adding too many branches to your tree, which will weaken it and stunt its growth.

To improve your learning, you must prune your tree by removing any irrelevant information (useless statistics, random anecdotes, pointless facts, meaningless examples, et cetera). Remember, what you need is a powerful, healthy tree, including the roots, the trunk, the branches and the foliage. You need a rock-solid understanding of key concepts. Then, and only then, can you start adding heavy decorations to your tree.

1

OVERCOMING INFORMATION OVERLOAD

A. Assessing how you consume information

The first step toward overcoming information overload is to observe the way you consume information. Are you binge-watching videos on YouTube? Are you reading article after article? Do you have too many unfinished books (or books you haven't even started)?

When your input (the information you absorb) is continuously greater than your output (what you do with the information), it creates a variety of issues such as:

* **Weak foundations.** You don't apply what you learn, so you don't really know anything at a deep level.
* **Information overload/analysis paralysis.** Having accumulated so much information, you don't know where to start. You simply can't filter out useful from irrelevant information.
* **Shiny Object Syndrome.** Being continuously exposed to new information, you often feel the desire to stop everything you do and start something else that sounds more exciting.
* **FOMO (fear of missing out).** You come across so many

"opportunities", you feel like you're constantly missing out on more exciting prospects.

- **Feelings of inadequacy.** Due to the way social media and other online content distorts reality, you hold onto unrealistic expectations. Everyone seems to be happier and more successful than you are. You start believing that something is wrong with you, which leads you to lose confidence and feel unworthy.

The point is, the more information you consume, the more problems you often have (unless you know where to find the right information).

I encourage you to spend time reflecting on the way you consume information. Do you spend a lot of time scrolling through your newsfeeds on social media? Do you watch too many videos on YouTube? Do you read too many articles, blogs or books?

B. Reducing the quantity of information you consume

By now, you should have a better idea of the amount of information you're consuming on a regular basis. In this section, we'll discuss what you can do to reduce your input of information so that you can focus more on the output. Below is a list of things you can do:

- **Unsubscribe from newsletters.** Most of the newsletters you subscribe to do not provide you with useful information that helps you reach your goals. Unsubscribe from them.
- **Spend less time on YouTube.** Similarly, most YouTube videos do not improve your life in any meaningful way, nor do they help you learn what you need to learn or move closer to your ideal self.
- **Remove phone notifications.** Interruptions kill your productivity and prevent you from doing deep work. All notifications on your phone, computer or any other device should be turned off unless they're vital.
- **Stay away from social media.** Social media is a huge distraction and often brings far less value than you think.

Limit your use of social media. Instead, meet people in real life. (Yes, people still do that.)

- **Read fewer articles.** Most articles aren't that interesting. They are too short to contain any real substance. Only focus on high-quality articles that are relevant to you.
- **Go on a news diet.** In most cases, you don't need to read the news every day. News clouds your judgment by giving you random facts taken out of context and without any depth or nuance. Instead, consider reading books (history, economics, or politics), which will provide you with a broader perspective, make you think deeper and help you make better decisions.
- **Go on an information diet.** When you feel overwhelmed or paralyzed, go on an information diet. Stop reading new articles. Don't buy any more books. Stay away from the news. Avoid YouTube and refrain from checking social media. Instead, only consume insightful material that you've already read before. Alternatively, focus on *creating* output.

Remember, in a world where information is abundant, your ability to sort it out and consume only what you need is an invaluable skill that will become increasingly important. It's not about quantity, it's about quality.

C. Web of knowledge vs. isolated facts

Some people know a lot of facts and would perform well in general knowledge quiz shows. However, does that mean they are deeply knowledgeable? Not necessarily. Learning isn't merely about remembering isolated facts, it's about learning key concepts and connecting them in a coherent way.

For instance, being a good student of history doesn't mean knowing thousands of historical dates. Knowing that the French Revolution occurred in 1789 isn't that useful per se. It's more important to understand the context in which it happened, such as:

- What events led to it?

- What was the political and economic situation at the time?
- Who were the main protagonists involved?
- What were the main reasons for the French Revolution?
- What were the key consequences?
- What changes occurred at the end of the French Revolution?

It's only when we understand the broader context and can explain it to someone that we can say we are truly knowledgeable. For most things we supposedly "know", we can't say that.

What about you? Do you have a solid web of knowledge covering various areas of your life, or is your mind filled with isolated facts you don't know what to do with?

For instance, perhaps:

- You know plenty of historical dates but are unable to grasp the major historical trends
- You memorized thousands of words in a foreign language, but can barely put a sentence together, or
- You understand some stoic principles, and may even have taken a Philosophy 101 class, but you can't explain key philosophical concepts

Now, there is nothing wrong with remembering facts or anecdotes, but you'll find it easier to remember them when they become part of a bigger web of knowledge. It will also make you a deeper thinker and better learner.

The bottom line is, when you consume too much information, you tend to remember a lot of irrelevant facts that do not make you more knowledgeable or any the wiser.

* * *

Action step

In your action guide, write down:

- The type of information you consume during a typical week
- What you'll do specifically to reduce the amount of information you consume

2

DESTROYING SHINY OBJECT SYNDROME

One of the main side effects of consuming too much information is what is referred to as Shiny Object Syndrome. This is when you keep jumping from one book, course, video or seminar to the next. As soon as you find something that looks more interesting or exciting than the course you're taking, you jump ship. This often leads you to spend years jumping from one thing to the next without achieving anything substantial.

Don't worry, though. We're going to work on solving that issue. Below are specific examples of Shiny Object Syndrome:

- Watching webinar after webinar and constantly trying new methods instead of establishing a clear business strategy and staying focused.
- Trying one learning language app after the other, hoping to find the magic bullet that will help you master your target language.
- Reading one book on learning after the next, hoping to find the "secret sauce" to learning.

A. The underlying beliefs behind Shiny Object Syndrome

People fall prey to Shiny Object Syndrome for specific reasons. Let's go over the main reasons behind this issue.

I. **FOMO (fear of missing out).** We are always on the lookout for opportunities. While there is nothing wrong with that, for many people, it stems from the inner belief that opportunities are scarce and will never represent themselves again.

This is rarely the case.

For instance, let's say you come across an online training course somewhat related to one of your goals. You discover it's on sale for only forty-eight hours. Afraid of missing out, you buy it. Here are the issues with this:

- You now have one more course to follow, which further clutters your mind.
- The course is not exactly what you need. Not being aligned with your current strategy, it scatters your focus and confuses you along the way.
- You wonder what to do with the course and how to integrate it with other courses or information you've already gathered.

The truth is that the fear of missing out is mostly an illusion. It comes from a place of lack—from the belief opportunities are scarce and limited. Sure, there may be opportunities you don't want to miss, but you should be highly skeptical and extremely picky when it comes to any new opportunity, whether it is an opportunity for:

- Fun (party, events)
- Learning (courses, training, books)
- New experiences (internships, travels, adventures), or
- Relationships (friendships, intimate relationships, networking)

Opportunities are everywhere. You just need to train yourself to notice them. Therefore, don't be afraid of missing out. Instead, be afraid of saying yes to the wrong ones.

2. Believing in the magic pill. Whether they're aware of it or not, many people are continuously looking for the magic pill—the one trick or strategy that will enable them to obtain the results they desire. Once you understand there is no magic pill that will make you fluent in a foreign language, allow you to become an expert in economics or help you master judo, you can focus on doing the job of learning.

If you tend to look for quick results or try to avoid doing hard work, you're probably looking for the magic pill.

3. Misunderstanding the learning cycle. When the progress they make doesn't match their expectations, many people start believing something is wrong with them. They worry that they aren't smart enough or talented enough to succeed. But this usually comes from a misunderstanding of how learning works. We don't make progress in a linear fashion—we make progress in a chaotic way. On some days, it may feel as though we're making great progress, whereas on others, it feels like we're getting worse. And sometimes we feel stuck for days or weeks barely making any progress (or at least, that's how it feels).

4. Lacking clarity. When you don't spend sufficient time clarifying your goals and creating a sound strategy, you become more likely to change your approach multiple times whenever you fail to see results, get bored or doubt the effectiveness of your actions.

That's why having an effective strategy is critical, as it will make it easy for you to stick to your original plan and keep learning until you obtain the desired results.

B. How to overcome Shiny Object Syndrome

Now that we've seen what Shiny Object Syndrome is and how it works, let's see what you can do specifically to immunize yourself against it.

1) Set fewer, more realistic goals. Most people try to learn too many things at once, so it's no wonder they begin to feel overwhelmed and fail to achieve the results they desire. Avoid having more than two, or a maximum of three, major learning goals at any one time. It's better to focus on a few things consistently and get results before moving on to other things, than to learn many things simultaneously and make little to no progress.

2) Make sure you are aligned with your goals. Choose disciplines or skills you're genuinely excited about learning, and make sure they align with your larger vision and values. The more aligned you are with your goals, the more likely you are to stick to them in the long term.

3) Have a sound strategy. Do your best to craft an effective strategy that will enable you to achieve your learning goals. This entails finding the right role models, identifying specific blueprints and creating an action plan that works for you.

4) Beware of FOMO. Stop trying to seize any new exciting "opportunity". Handpick a few disciplines or skills you're excited to learn about and accept you can't learn everything. Whenever you feel the urge to consume more information or try something new, ask yourself whether it's strictly necessary. Chances are that you're better off sticking to your original plan.

Years ago, after having identified a clear blueprint, I committed to keep writing books until I made a full-time income. It wasn't easy. There were dozens of times when I felt like doing something else, whether creating courses, coaching or trying out a shiny new strategy. However, every time I would tell myself, "All I need to do is to keep writing"—and I did.

It's a good example of how Shiny Object Syndrome is always lurking around in the background. You'll be tempted many times. The question is, will you stick to your original strategy, or will you get distracted at the first opportunity?

C. When is Shiny Object Syndrome useful

Jumping from one thing to the next isn't always a bad idea. Sometimes, you should adjust your strategy or try different things. However, you must be certain that you're doing it for the right reasons and at the right time.

Before deciding to try something new, ask yourself whether your existing strategy is still relevant. It may be suboptimal or ineffective for several reasons:

- **It may not be working.** It is possible that even when applied effectively, your current learning strategy is just not working for you. If so, go back to the drawing board and try to create a better plan.
- **It may be uninspiring.** Even though your existing learning strategy might be highly effective, you might find yourself unable to follow it. If you lack motivation and feel uninspired, remember why you wanted to learn that skill or discipline in the first place. Does the reason still hold true? If you can't find strong emotional reasons to learn it, it may not be the right thing for you to learn right now.
- **It may be unrealistic for *you*.** It may also be that your learning plan is just too complicated or too demanding, either because you designed it that way or because your personal situation has changed, leaving you with less time and energy than expected. If so, you might need to adjust your learning plan accordingly.

One caveat though. Avoid dropping your goals for the following reasons:

- **Fear.** Dropping a goal because your priorities have changed is fine but doing so because you are scared isn't. Ask yourself, "Do I want to give up because of fear or because my priorities and interests have genuinely changed?"
- **Lack of progress.** We often make progress but don't notice it.

Keep going until you reach a new breakthrough or revise your strategy when needed. Ask yourself, "Is my progress slower because I'm about to reach a new level or because my current strategy is ineffective?" Note that it is also possible you're making progress without realizing it.

PART V

THE DIFFERENT TYPES OF LEARNING

Now that we've reviewed some of the most effective learning tools and techniques, and have discussed how to overcome common traps such as information overload and Shiny Object Syndrome, let's look at the different types of learning. Depending upon the nature of your learning, the techniques and methods you'll need will vary. In this section, we'll take an in-depth look at four different types of learning and see what you can do specifically to maximize your results for each.

These four types of learning are:

1. Conceptual learning
2. Practical skills learning
3. Language learning, and
4. Learning for tests and exams

But before we do that, it's important we discuss the two main systems our brain relies on to learn anything new. These two systems are often used collectively, but one or the other will be used more extensively depending on the type of learning you're engaging in. These two systems are:

- The declarative system, and
- The procedural system

The declarative system

Put simply, the declarative system is the system you rely on to learn things by heart or in a step-by-step fashion. It's a conscious process. For instance, you rely on the declarative system to:

- Learn new vocabulary, conjugation and definitions of concepts
- Solve math problems, and
- Follow a step-by-step course or specific instructions

The procedural system

The procedural system is the system that enables you to recognize and internalize new patterns. As opposed to the declarative system, the procedural system is mostly unconscious, and happens automatically. You mainly rely on this system when you learn practical skills such as sports, cooking, driving or playing a musical instrument. Procedural learning is the process that enables you to transfer a skill from your conscious to your subconscious.

The following table summarizes the main differences between the two systems.

	Declarative system	Procedural system
Level of control	Conscious	Mostly unconscious
Input	Working memory	Senses
Type of learning	Involves cognitive tasks	Involves motor skills
Modus operandi	Step-by-step explanations	Pattern recognition/building

Now, why should you know about these two systems?

Because, based on the type of learning you do, they'll have to be used differently and to different degrees.

For example, when learning a foreign language, many people spend all their time remembering vocabulary by using flashcards (declarative system). However, a foreign language isn't merely something you learn by heart like a poem. It's made up of hundreds or thousands of different patterns. We must learn different tenses, and when to use them. We must learn conjugations. We must be able to use grammatical forms to construct sentences that reflect our thinking correctly, and so on. The only way to internalize all these patterns is by making effective use of the procedural system, which entails speaking to actual people in real life, or consuming loads of content, as we'll discuss in the upcoming section on language learning.

To oversimplify, we can say that declarative learning is used for abstract learning (cognitive skills), while the procedural system is used for practical learning (motor skills). Understanding when and how to use the declarative and procedural systems, will help you learn more effectively.

Now, let's deep dive into the four main types of learning and see what the most effective ways are to approach each one.

	Conceptual learning	Practical skills	Language learning	Standardized tests
Motto	Build solid foundations	Practice, practice, practice	Make mistakes but keep going	Do as you are told
Method	Start with the big picture	Identify the most effective blueprint	Speak in real life situations / consume tons of content	Gather official guidebooks and relevant materials
Main idea	Master key concepts/laws/ principles	Practice deliberately	Immerse yourself	Answer all previous test questions

1

CONCEPTUAL LEARNING

The first type of learning is conceptual learning. It includes disciplines like philosophy, economics or politics as well as everything else that requires the understanding of numerous concepts.

Below are some key characteristics of conceptual learning:

- It relies heavily on declarative learning and less on procedural learning.
- It entails grasping new concepts, laws or mental models to increase your web of knowledge.
- It requires a great deal of cognitive effort and limited physical effort.

For conceptual learning, you can apply most of the effective learning techniques we mentioned previously, such as recalling, elaborating or spaced repetition. Teaching is probably the most effective method to develop conceptual learning as it entails applying many of the above learning methods.

How to learn conceptual skills

Master the fundamentals

To become a master at conceptual learning, you must build solid foundations (a thick tree trunk on top of healthy roots), which requires you to grasp key concepts and understand the most important laws, theories or mental models in the field you seek to build expertise in.

One way to ensure you're learning is to test yourself on any major key concepts or pieces of information that you deem essential. For instance, you can:

- Write down your own definition of key concepts and then compare them to the actual definitions.
- Give specific examples to illustrate important concepts, laws or mental models.
- Teach key concepts to your friends, classmates or colleagues. Alternatively, you can write an article or record a video about it.
- When relevant, apply the concepts in real life.
- Summarize chapters or passages of a book in your own words.
- Reread foundational materials and test yourself until you have truly mastered them.

Remember, we know far less than we think we do. It's likely that your knowledge on a variety of topics is incomplete or superficial. To test your knowledge, explain what you know to a friend and see how well you can explain it.

For instance:

- If you're studying physics, try to explain to a friend, in layman's terms, the most important theories and laws you've studied so far.
- If you're learning economics, select a few concepts that you're not sure you understand well and teach them to a

friend or summarize them in a way that a six-year-old can understand. Then, go back to your course material, study more and repeat the process several times if necessary.

- If you're struggling to solve a certain type of math problem, keep solving similar problems until you understand the concept and the process.

This process can be tedious, so you may not want to do it all the time. However, for anything you're serious about learning, keep playing with the key concepts you want to internalize until you can teach them to anyone with confidence and relative ease.

Go from general to specific

When we learn, we often get lost at some point in the process. Overwhelmed by too much new information, we lose track of key ideas while remembering small details of little importance. For any skill that fits into the conceptual learning category, train yourself to prioritize the information. Zoom out of the detail and ask yourself what's truly important. The better you understand the fundamentals, the stronger your tree trunk and root system will be, and the more deeply you'll be able to learn by adding more branches to your tree. You shouldn't be afraid to spend a disproportionate amount of time learning the basics. It's not about learning more or faster; it's about deepening your understanding and building new mental models.

Start with accessible content

Whenever you try to learn a new concept, instead of starting with a 300-page book on the topic or a twenty-page article, start with the simplest and easiest-to-understand piece of content you can find. It will give you an overall picture of what you're trying to learn, while preventing you from feeling overwhelmed and getting lost in the details.

For instance, run a quick search online. Then, look for short, accessible content. Wikipedia might be a good place to start. Usually, it offers a brief definition of the concept at the top of the page before diving into greater detail. Perhaps content for kids might be helpful. The key point is that you should gain a basic understanding of what the subject is about, what it may be used for or how you can apply it in your life.

Look for specific examples

The next step is to look for specific examples. The more examples you have that illustrate a concept, the easier it will be to understand. Here is a good analogy: in Japanese, many words have no direct translation in English. This is because they represent concepts that simply don't exist in other countries or cultures. The only way to understand them is to be exposed to the concept in various contexts until you finally internalize them.

Similarly, knowing in what context a concept is used in together with several specific examples can help deepen your understanding and build a better mental representation of the overall concept.

Come up with your own examples

A good sign that you understand a concept is your ability to provide specific examples, metaphors or analogies. Therefore, whenever you try to recall a model, try to recall specific examples that were given when you studied it. Then, strive to develop your own examples or metaphors. Do the same when you teach or summarize a topic.

Expand your personal library of mental models

The more mental models you internalize, the faster you can acquire new ones. This is because mental models give you a bigger receptacle to hold more knowledge. They enable you to make parallels, connect new concepts with previous ones and come up with different examples and analogies more easily. Great thinkers and learners have internalized thousands of mental models. As a result, they have a solid tree trunk upon which they can keep adding more knowledge.

Here is what you can do to build your library of mental models:

- **Read more.** The more you read, the more mental models you will pick up over time. Also, strive to read books on various topics to expand your knowledge base and pick up new ways of thinking. Don't neglect fiction. Novels are a great way to see life through the minds of a variety of people who live or have lived in different places and times.

- **Study mental models specifically.** There are books and blogs that introduce you to some of the most useful mental models. For instance, Shane Parrish and Rhiannon Beaubien have written a series of three books on mental models called, *The Great Mental Models*. Shane Parrish also runs a blog at https://fs.blog called, *Helping you master the best of what other people have already figured out.*
- **Become aware of the concept of "mental models".** Just by reading this book and gaining a better understanding of what mental models actually are, you'll be able to spot them more easily and make a conscious effort to internalize them as you continue learning.
- **Learn how to learn.** Make sure you have a solid foundation from which to begin your learning, by reading books such as this.
- **Acquire key concepts in several disciplines.** Build strong fundamentals. The more concepts you know, the more concepts you can acquire, and the more readily you will acquire them.

Use the Feynman Technique

Another way to reinforce your learning is to apply the Feynman Technique. Named after the Nobel Prize-winning physicist, Richard Feynman, this technique consists of five simple steps:

- **Choose a concept.** First, select a concept you want to work on, take a sheet of paper and write it at the top.
- **Explain it.** Explain the idea as though you need to teach it to someone else. To do so, make sure you use your own words, write simply and challenge yourself to come up with a couple of examples. To make it even more effective, imagine yourself teaching it to a kid. To paraphrase Albert Einstein,

"If you can't teach it to a six-years-old, you probably don't understand it that well."

- **Identify the gaps in your understanding.** As you strive to explain the concept in your own words, you'll notice where you fall short. That's one of the main benefits of this method —it instantly throws light on things you don't understand.
- **Go back to the source material and review.** Now that you have identified your areas of weakness, revisit your learning material one more time and review it. When needed, seek other materials that will help you deepen your understanding of the concept.
- **Simplify.** Finally, explain the concept one more time in the simplest way possible.

Writing down key concepts using this method is a great way to learn. As I tweeted a while ago: "Honest writing is simple because it has nothing to hide. Dishonest writing is complex because it tries to hide its real intentions, insufficient understanding of the topic or unrefined thinking."

The point is, to write simply requires you to think well, as does learning. Because writing demands that you sharpen your thinking, it also makes you a better learner in the process.

2

PRACTICAL SKILLS

Now let's consider the most effective way to learn practical skills. By practical skills, I mean everything that involves using your body in some way. While conceptual learning only requires that you use your intellect, practical skills rely on both your intellect *and* the coordination of a variety of physical actions. This goes for any sport or any craft you want to learn.

In this instance, learning requires you to practice specific moves repeatedly until they become second nature. Earlier, we talked about procedural learning and explained how it is linked to the repetition of physical moves. To learn any craft, you'll have to rely heavily on this type of learning until your subconscious can perform the thousands of moves required to master your craft. As previously explained, I refer to this process as "transferring a skill to your subconscious". Driving is a good example. Remember your first driving lesson? There were so many things to think about simultaneously that you probably felt overwhelmed. However, with practice, driving has become almost automatic. Now, you can listen to music or talk with your friends while driving. You have effectively transferred the skill of driving a car to your subconscious.

Below are the key characteristics of practical learning:

- It relies heavily on procedural learning (transferring a skill to your subconscious).
- It must be learned mostly by doing.
- It requires a great deal of repetition and plenty of practice.

A. Mastering procedural learning

Doing is key to acquiring any practical skill. One of the most common mistakes people make is spending too much time thinking or "studying" instead of doing. Remember, you can only make real progress by having 'skin in the game', which in most cases simply means doing the very same thing you want to master. For instance, if you:

- Want to become a better driver? Ddrive.
- Want to improve your karate skills? Practice punches and kicks.
- Want to become a skilled cook? Follow many cooking recipes.

The point is, you must take the most effective action possible, which usually involves being in a real-life situation.

Another way to think of the concept of "having skin in the game" is being willing to expose yourself to so-called failures and other people's judgments.

For instance, if you attend cooking classes, you may completely fail a recipe and fear other participants will make fun of you. You may also compare yourself to others, which makes things worse. If you organize a dinner, you're also exposing yourself to the risk of "failing". What if your recipe isn't as tasty as you thought? What if your guests hate your dishes? What will they think of you?

Alternatively, imagine you want to learn karate and you join a dojo in your area. At first, it might be uncomfortable. You might feel out of place and awkward, but that's the price you must pay to learn karate and become an expert in the long term.

Every time you refuse to have skin in the game, you slow your progress, which is why most people are slow learners. They hope to replace hard work with books, videos or seminars, trying to intellectualize their way to success. But the truth is that, to transfer a skill to your subconscious, you must practice, practice and practice even more. The closer that practice is to the real-life situation, the better.

Note that practicing doesn't mean you have to make a fool of yourself from the very beginning. What Tim Ferris refers to as "no stakes practice" is also an effective way to dip your toe in the water and familiarize yourself with the skill or set of skills you're trying to learn.

For instance, you can:

- Film yourself giving a speech without showing it to anyone. That way, you can practice delivering speeches with the minimal pressure.
- Practice cooking skills at home. That way, you don't feel pressured to make the perfect dish.
- Journaling or writing a blog that almost nobody reads. That way, you're less likely to feel judged by people.

In fact, for many skills, the number of hours you spend practicing by yourself is one of the best predictors of success. For instance, a study conducted in the early nineties at the Music Academy of West Berlin showed that the main difference between the best violinists and the rest wasn't how much time they dedicated to music-related group activities (lessons, practice or classes), but how much time they spent practicing by themselves; the two groups of violinists rated as excellent and very good by their professors engaged in solo practice twenty-four hours a week on average while a third group practiced only nine hours a week.

B. How to learn practical skills

Some people are natural action takers. However, oftentimes, acting isn't enough. You must also act the right way. Practice doesn't make perfect. We all know people who "practice" for years without improving much. Meanwhile, we also know people who improve at an impressive rate in a matter of months. The main reason is that they practice *effectively and with the right mindset*.

In this section, we'll see how you can improve your practice. More specifically, we'll cover the how to:

1. Set specific goals
2. Identify the best blueprint or training
3. Create a schedule
4. Break down the skill into relevant sub-skills
5. Practice deliberately

Step 1: Set specific goals

Before you start learning any practical skills, you must clarify your learning goals (if necessary, revisit the section on how to set specific goals). The reason is simple: you cannot move to the next step unless you know exactly what you're trying to learn. If you want to become the best in the world, you'll probably need to train differently compared to if you're merely learning something for enjoyment.

Consequently, make sure you define your goals. That is:

- Find compelling reasons to learn the skill. The stronger your why, the more likely you are to stay committed to your goal over the longer term. Remember, passion is the most effective learning driver available.
- Ensure your goal is aligned with your vision and values (whenever possible). When your goals are connected to your values and your overall vision, you'll find it much easier to remain committed.
- Set a SMART goal. The more specific your goals are, the easier it will be to build an effective action plan.

Step 2: Identify the best blueprint or training

In most cases, there are people before you who have either learned the exact same skill, or a very similar one. These individuals paved the way. All you need to do is to find out how they did it. Of course, just because someone has learned something doesn't mean they learned it in the most optimal way possible. Therefore, you should make sure that you find people who:

1. Are the best at what they do, and
2. Have shared the method, blueprint or training they used

Because your time is limited, you simply can't afford to reinvent the wheel.

How to find the best blueprint

To create your learning blueprint, you can:

- Ask people for help
- Do your own research
- Buy materials from the best experts/coaches
- Hire a coach, and/or
- Find a mentor

Since we've already explained how to find the best blueprint earlier, let's go over each point briefly.

1) Ask people for help

Whenever I want to learn something new or need some information on a topic, I always ask myself who can help me out among the people I know. Consequently, ask yourself if you know someone who has already learned what you want to learn.

2) Do your own research

Once you've asked friends or acquaintances for help or advice, start gathering relevant content. Do any additional research needed. Find the best experts and teachers, and so on.

3) Buy materials from the best experts/coaches

Look for the best books, products or courses that will provide you with the step-by-step method you need to reach your learning goal.

Note that it isn't always necessary to buy books or products, or work with coaches. You can use free resources online, but it will be harder to pull materials together to create an effective blueprint. Purchasing high-quality materials or hiring a coach may help you by:

- Giving you a well-organized step-by-step method that you can start using immediately. Having structured content will prevent you wasting your time and energy gathering the relevant resources. Nothing is free. The time you spend looking for high-quality free resources and organizing them could have been better spent elsewhere. Having a structure to follow also reduces the risk that you will encounter erroneous information, and it will make it easy for you to create an effective learning plan. For instance, a coach might provide you with a customized plan that meets your needs.
- Motivating you to act. As the saying goes, "When you pay, you pay attention." Investing your hard-earned money means you'll probably take things more seriously, and as a result, you will be more consistent and more committed.

Step 3: Create a schedule

Once you have identified the best blueprint, you must create an effective learning schedule. Having a specific schedule will enable you to stay consistent with your learning. Consistency is usually far more powerful than intensity. Once you've built consistency, you can increase intensity.

How to create an effective and efficient learning schedule

Let's review a few specific things you can do to create an effective learning schedule. As the author and productivity expert, Michael Hyatt, said, "what gets scheduled, gets done".

1) Decide how many hours to study

The first step is to decide how many hours per week you'll spend practicing or studying. Remember that to develop any major skill, you should ideally dedicate *at least* three to five hours per week.

2) Block time on your calendar

When it comes to productivity, one of the most effective methods is to block time in your calendar. Blocking time is akin to making an appointment with yourself. This means you should show up on time and take your practice as seriously as you would take a doctor's appointment.

The simplest way to block time might be to use an online calendar. You can also use a physical calendar.

When you block time for regular practice, avoid changing it and try to have a regular schedule each week. This will allow you to develop a routine, which will boost your productivity and improve your focus.

Step 4: Break down the skill into relevant sub-skills

Break down your learning goal into various sub-skills you can then work on separately and master. A better word for it might be to "deconstruct" the skill you want to learn.

For instance, in *The Art of Learning*, professional chess player Josh Waitzkin explains how, in his early study of chess, he reduced the complexity by focusing only on one small aspect of the game: *"I explored endgame positions of reduced complexity—for example king and pawn against king, only three pieces on the board—in order to touch high-level principles such as the power of empty space,* zugzwang *(where any move of the opponent will destroy his position), tempo, or structural planning."* This enabled him to develop mental frameworks on a variety of situations during chess matches later in his career.

You can also consider martial arts students. At first, they don't practice complicated moves. Instead, they keep practicing basic punches and kicks thousands of times. This concept of learning the fundamentals and revising them over and over is key to mastering any skill.

Isolating skills

Deconstructing a skill into its main sub-skills can also be useful when you've reached a plateau. Often, this happens when something is acting as a bottleneck.

As Geoff Colvin wrote in *Talent is Overrated*, "*The great performers isolate remarkably specific aspects of what they do and focus on just those things until they are improved; then it's on to the next aspect.*"

For example, look at Tiger Woods. He hired a coach to help him improve his swing. Yes, the best golfer in the world went back to the fundamentals to step his game to the next level.

Or as Nick Velasquez says in *Learn, Improve, Master*, "*Even the great swimmer Michael Phelps, would do practice drills using just his arms and legs [...] By deconstructing a style and isolating parts of it in this practice, Phelps could find what was holding him back and work on it.*"

Interestingly, Tiger Woods and Michael Phelps' situations are not uncommon. Many world-class athletes return to the basics to optimize their performance.

The bottom line is, to improve, you must identify what's limiting you, and work on it consciously. Unless you shed the light on your weaknesses, you won't develop your strengths and you won't improve.

For instance:

- You may be a good tennis player, but perhaps your serve isn't accurate or powerful enough. If so, focus on improving your serve.
- You may type quite fast but perhaps struggle with certain keys. Let's say the "X" key causes you trouble. If so, practice hitting this key over and over. Go back and forth between the starting hand positions and the positions needed to hit the "X" key. Then, practice typing words with the letter "X". Finally, write full sentences.
- You may be a good poker player, but you can't seem to go to the next level because you lose your temper occasionally. If

so, work on your mindset, perhaps by practicing meditation or working with a psychology coach.

In summary, to enhance your performance, practice important moves or techniques you may be struggling with until you transfer them effectively to your subconscious. Remember, if you do not identify what's limiting you and work on it proactively, you'll remain stuck. That's what happens to most people. Accordingly, for any skill you wish to master, actively try to improve—always. This leads us to our next point.

Step 5—Practice deliberately

The key to becoming more proficient at any skill is to be intentional with your practice. Just practicing for the sake of it, even if you spend years doing so, will never enable you to master your craft. Soon, you'll reach a plateau—and you'll likely stay there forever.

Various studies have shown that most people stop improving past a certain point. For instance, according to researchers at Harvard Medical School, doctors with decades of experience don't seem to provide better patient care than those with just a few years of experience. And studies have shown similar results in many other professions.

When people say they have twenty years of experience, what they truly say is that they learned for the first three years before being on autopilot for the remaining seventeen. Conversely, people who rely on deliberate practice never stop improving. They keep adding new mental models and continually refine key movements and techniques. The only way they can do so is by practicing consciously.

How to practice deliberately

To practice deliberately, you must implement proven training methods and challenge yourself on specific well-defined goals that require your full attention and provide you with regular feedback.

In their book, *Peak, Secrets from The New Science of Expertise*, Anders Ericsson and Robert Pool identified several key factors that make for deliberate practice. According to them, deliberate practice:

- Builds skills for which effective training techniques already exist
- Requires significant effort and is generally not enjoyable
- Involves specific, well-defined goals
- Requires full concentration
- Provides regular feedback
- Enables you to develop effective mental representation, and
- Usually involves working on existing skills (or developing new ones) by focusing on the specific aspects you need to improve

Let's elaborate on each of these briefly by using tennis as an example.

1) Deliberate practice builds skills for which effective training techniques already exist.

Chances are the goal you are trying to reach has already been achieved by someone else. As such, there is no need to reinvent the wheel.

If you wish to become a professional tennis player, why not copy the practices used by people who have already reached that status? This might entail hiring a coach, reading sports magazines or watching training videos on YouTube.

Sometimes however, the path toward your goal is unclear. Perhaps there isn't a proven method to achieve your goal. If so, do some research and design your own blueprint. You can always refine it over time.

2) Deliberate practice requires significant effort and is generally not enjoyable.

If you keep doing the things you already know how to do, your progress will slow, and you'll eventually reach a plateau, being unable to improve your performance.

Playing tennis with your friends every Sunday might be fun, but how much progress can you reasonably make? On the other hand, practicing your serve for two hours is tedious, but when done right, will turn you into a better player.

However, I wouldn't go as far as saying deliberate practice is "not enjoyable". In fact, working on a challenging task can actually increase the odds we reach a state of flow—i.e., a mental state in which we're so fully immersed in an activity that we become hyper-focused while experiencing a sense of underlying enjoyment.

3) Deliberate practice involves specific, well-defined goals.

Working on your first serve is a specific and well-defined goal. Playing with your friends on Sundays isn't, since you probably won't be working on a specific skill, you'll just be having fun.

For each deliberate practice session, set a clear goal and be intentional about it. This will make a massive difference in the way you practice.

4) Deliberate practice requires full concentration.

If you practice serves with focus, you will improve. However, if you go through the motions mechanically—as you would when washing the dishes—your progress will be slower, and you'll reach a plateau very quickly.

Remember, deliberate practice can never be something you do on autopilot. If what you do doesn't require your full concentration, then you're probably not practicing deliberately enough. You might be inside your comfort zone doing things you already know how to do well.

5) Deliberate practice provides you with regular feedback.

As you practice your first serve, you receive instant feedback on the results. In addition, if you work with a coach, they will point out what you need to focus on to improve. As you make adjustments based on that feedback, you will almost inevitably improve.

6) Deliberate practice enables you to develop effective mental representation.

Through deliberate practice and repetition, you create a mental representation of patterns of information that will be held in long-term memory. These patterns contain various elements—facts, images, rules, muscle memories or relationships—organized in a coherent way. Deliberate practice allows you to create effective mental representations which, in turn, boost your performance. For instance, mental representation allows taxi drivers to find their routes in complex cities, and enables chess masters to play blindfolded.

A tennis player who has practiced the same move repeatedly will have a far more effective mental representation of the action than someone who plays tennis as a hobby.

7) Deliberate practice usually involves working on existing skills (or developing new ones) by focusing on specific aspects to improve.

When you play tennis with your friends on Sunday, you're generally not trying to improve any specific skill. You may improve your game slightly over time, but your progress is likely to be slow and rather random.

On the other hand, when you apply deliberate practice, you break down a skill or a craft into its different components. Tennis can be seen as one skill that encompasses a whole set of other skills. Some of those skills are first serve, second serve, forehand, backhand, volley, footwork and so on. If we further break down these macro skills, sub-skills might involve isolating a muscle via a well-defined exercise to improve a certain shot or practicing a specific exercise to increase your stamina.

Therefore, if you want to improve, identify a few key sub-skills and work on them deliberately and consistently until you see some improvement. Remember to use distributed and interleaved practice for greater effectiveness. For instance, practice different types of serves during your practice session and make sure you practice as consistently as possible.

The bottom line is, for practical skills, identify the best blueprint (or create one). Then, use deliberate practice to ensure that your learning is highly effective.

Regular practice vs. deliberate practice

If you practice like everyone else, you'll never reach a high level of expertise. Practice does not make perfect. Only "perfect" practice makes perfect.

In this section, we'll spend time exploring what "perfect" practice means.

The main problem with the way most people practice

How come some people can practice for years and see only marginal improvement, while others can make massive progress in a matter of months? Is it due to innate talent, hard work, or exceptional discipline? Or is there something else?

To try to understand, let's have a look at the world-class juggler Laido Dittmar. His story is particularly enlightening.

Laido Dittmar is one of the four people in the entire world who can juggle with eleven rings simultaneously. However, this is not the most interesting thing about him.

What's interesting is that he only started juggling when he was seventeen years old—or over a decade later than most professional jugglers. Imagine being ten years behind in terms of practice. Assuming professional jugglers practice three hours a day on average, that's over 10,000 hours of practice he needed to catch up on. It's a little like being on the starting line of a marathon while others are about to cross the finishing line.

After a couple of years of intense practice, he was still nowhere near becoming a professional juggler. If anything, he was laughed at and told that he had no talent, that he started too late and that he was trying the impossible. Despite practicing sometimes for eight hours a day, five days a week, his progress was slow, and there was no sign of a future world-class juggler.

So, how did he become world class?

Put simply, he changed the way he practiced. By observing the best performers in the world, he discovered a simple "secret":

World-class performers spend most of their time practicing moves and techniques that fall beyond their comfort zone. Meanwhile, average people spend most of their time trying to polish existing skills.

Now, one of the reasons most people do not practice effectively is because they hold onto the following assumptions:

1. If I don't practice what I've learned before, I'll lose the skill.
2. I must master a skill completely before moving on to something more challenging.

These two assumptions are dangerous, and deserve spending a little time exploring them in more detail.

Assumption #1: If I don't practice what I've learned before, I'll lose the skill.

Many people are more afraid of losing than they are interested in winning. This is a common bias called "aversion loss". This bias is also reflected in the way people practice. Unconsciously, people believe that if they do not practice something enough times, they will forget it. As a result, they spend most of their practice time reviewing what they already know how to do fairly well.

- Musicians play the same songs they've already played dozens of times.
- Tennis players practice the same serves over and over.
- Soccer players practice the same dribbling techniques again and again.

The issue is, once they've practiced what they already know, they have little time and energy left to practice new challenging skills that will truly enable them to improve.

To simplify, we can say that average performers spend the first 80% of their practice session working on old stuff, and the last 20% working on new challenging stuff. On the other hand, world-class performers spend the first 80% practicing new challenging stuff and the last 20% working on old stuff.

Yes, mastering the fundamentals is key. But we must alternate between strengthening the fundamentals and challenging ourselves. It's the constant tension between practicing something a little outside our comfort zone at the beginning of each session, and going back to the fundamentals toward the end of it that enables us to make continuous progress.

In other words, world class performers:

- Spend most of their time practicing moves or techniques somewhat beyond their comfort zone, and
- Do so at the beginning of their practice session when they have the most energy available

Meanwhile, average performers:

- Only spend a minority of their time on challenging moves or techniques, and
- Do so at the end of their practice session when they have little energy left.

As a result, world-class performers improve at a much faster rate. The additional time they spend on challenging stuff combined with the high energy level they can put into their practice dramatically enhances the effectiveness of their training. This is how Laido Dittmar was able to catch up and become one of the best jugglers in the world.

Assumption #2: I must master a skill completely before moving on to something more challenging.

The other reason most people do not challenge themselves enough is that they believe they're not ready yet. They see practice as a video game with different levels to clear, and they can only move on to the next level when they feel as though they've completed the level they're currently at.

The problem is the brain doesn't work that way. It doesn't think in terms of levels. To make rapid progress, the brain needs to be forced to adapt to challenging conditions. In other words, you must practice beyond your comfort zone to create new neural connections and expand your field of competence. You must force your brain to grow.

Realize that, whenever you practice, there is a trade-off between polishing your existing skills and practicing new, more challenging ones. The countless hours you put into trying to get to the last five or ten percent of a skill could have been spent practicing another move or technique that is currently beyond your comfort zone.

The power of stretching

As Ralph Waldo Emerson wrote, *"The mind, once stretched by a new idea, never returns to its original dimensions."*

This also seems to be the case with our brain. Whenever we practice a skill that is a little beyond our comfort zone, we stretch our brain and develop new abilities.

You might think that if you move to the next "level" without having cleared the level you're currently at, you won't be able to master any skills to execute them flawlessly. However, here is the trick: after you stretch yourself for a while, go back to practicing the skill you haven't completely mastered yet. In most cases, you'll find out that it has become easier. The reason for this is probably because:

- You've attempted to do even harder things that have stretched your brain. In the process, you've acquired new skills that have helped you improve your overall performance.
- You've given your subconscious time to consolidate existing neural connections. By concentrating on another technique rather than trying to polish an existing skill, you're taking a mini-break and practicing a sort of spaced repetition.

For instance, When Laido Dittmar could juggle with four rings fairly well, but not consistently, he started practicing with five rings. When he returned to juggling with four rings, he found it much easier. Then, he kept practicing the same way until, eventually, he could juggle with eleven rings.

The bottom line is, to improve, you must constantly challenge yourself. This is why people tend to make progress fast whenever they pick up a new skill. Since everything is new, their brain has no choice but to adapt. However, soon enough, they fall into the trap of practicing what they already know fairly well, instead of learning new techniques that lie beyond their comfort zone.

To sum up:

1. Practice challenging things first when you have the most energy.
2. Review current skills at the end of the practice session when you have little energy left.

Main takeaways:

To learn any practical skills, you must be on the "battlefield". You must have skin in the game. Therefore, always strive to have more skin in the game, not less. This entails exposing yourself to temporary failures, being judged by others and being envious of people who are currently much better than you.

Follow the steps below to acquire practical skills:

- **Set a specific goal.** Before you start learning any practical skills, spend time clarifying your learning goals. To do so, find compelling reasons to learn it, ensure it is aligned with your vision and values, and set a SMART goal.
- **Identify the best blueprint and training.** People before you have already learned the exact same skill or a very similar one. Find out how they did it by asking people for help, doing your own research, buying books or courses, hiring a

coach and/or finding a mentor. There is no need to reinvent the wheel.

- **Create a schedule.** Having a specific schedule will enable you to stay consistent with your learning, which will accumulate over time. Consistency is usually far more powerful than intensity. Once you've built consistency, you can increase intensity. To create a learning schedule, decide how many hours you'll study each week, and make an appointment with yourself by blocking time in your calendar.
- **Break down (deconstruct) the skills into relevant sub-skills.** Break down your learning goal into various sub-skills you can work on separately and master. Make sure to practice fundamental moves and techniques over and over (while challenging yourself to learn new ones). This is key to mastering any skill.
- **Practice deliberately.** To become an expert at any skill, you must be "intentional" with your practice. Practicing for the sake of it, even if you spend years doing so, will never enable you to master your craft. Consequently, never stop improving using the concept of deliberate practice. That is, implement proven training methods and challenge yourself with specific well-defined goals that require your full attention and provide you with regular feedback.

* * *

Action step

Using your action guide, write down what deliberate practice would look like specifically for one of your goals.

3

LANGUAGE LEARNING

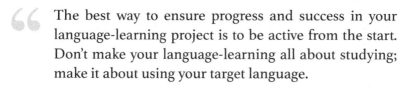 The best way to ensure progress and success in your language-learning project is to be active from the start. Don't make your language-learning all about studying; make it about using your target language.

— BENNY LEWIS, AUTHOR OF *FLUENT IN 3 MONTHS*.

For mysterious reasons, many people seem to believe they can't become fluent in a foreign language. Perhaps they think they're too old, learning languages isn't their thing, or they're just not smart enough. What I like to remind myself of is that, if over a billion people can learn Chinese, I can too. You might argue that most of them learned it when they were young, and that's true. Kids are definitely better at learning languages, but that doesn't mean we can't learn languages later in life.

I started learning new languages when I was seventeen. Five years later, I was in a classroom in Tokyo, listening to a teacher reading Aristotle's work out loud—in Japanese. My English was also pretty good. However, I did spend an incredible amount of time studying these languages.

The point is, learning foreign languages does take time, but if you're learning the right way and staying consistent, like everything else, you'll eventually become really good at it. Another way to demystify learning foreign languages is to realize that a language is nothing more than:

- Words to remember, and
- A set of limited grammatical rules

You already know tens of thousands of words in your native language. Picking up a few thousand more but in another language isn't a big deal and grammatical rules are finite. You've learned far more rules in science and other topics. At some point, you'll have learned most of the grammatical rules needed to speak fluently, and with practice, it will become almost automatic. Your subconscious will do most of the hard work for you.

Below are some key characteristics of language learning:

- It relies both on declarative learning and procedural learning, and
- To be truly effective, it requires consistency.

Now, let's see what specific methods you can use to learn foreign languages effectively.

In this book, I've highlighted two learning methods, which I believe you'll benefit a great deal from using. I call these methods "direct learning" and "input learning".

In direct learning, you'll be speaking from day one. This is the method the polyglot, Benny Lewis, recommends in his book, *Fluent in 3 Months*.

With input learning, you'll be consuming a lot of content to immerse yourself in the language (video, audio, text). You'll only begin to speak when you understand the language quite well. This is the method recommended by the YouTuber, Matt vs. Japan.

Let's explain each method in more detail, shall we?

A. Direct learning

The main characteristic of this method is that you start speaking from day one. You'll make tons of mistakes, but it doesn't matter, because every mistake moves you closer to fluency.

It's the opposite of what most people do, and it's the opposite of how we learned languages at school. With a decent learning method, everybody should be able to speak a foreign language fairly well after seven years of study. However, after learning English in France for seven years, except for basic conversations, most students are unable to speak English when they graduate from high school.

Who is direct learning for?

This method is for everybody who wants to learn to speak a foreign language relatively quickly (in a few months). You can also use it to reach a high level of fluency. However, the second method we'll discuss later will be more efficient, but only if you truly want to master a language and are willing to put in the required number of hours.

Let's see in detail how direct learning works.

1) Speak from day one

There is no authority or gatekeeper preventing you from speaking any language at any time. Therefore, begin to speak the language you want to learn as soon as possible. In his book, *Fluent in 3 Months*, Benny Lewis recommends that we start speaking from the very first day even if it's just a few words. He teaches that the earlier we put ourselves in the "language arena", the better.

Speaking from day one without worrying about grammar might sound difficult for many people. One of the main reasons is that it entails making mistakes—a lot of mistakes. When I started studying English and Japanese, I was terrified of making mistakes. I wanted each sentence to be grammatically correct and was worried about my pronunciation. Most of this has to do with the way we've been taught at school to approach "mistakes" and "failures". We've been conditioned to fear mistakes. However, that's just not how real learning works. So-called mistakes and failures are inherent to the learning process and cannot be avoided.

A healthier way to deal with "failures" is to see them for what they truly are: "feedback". Every mistake you make is feedback from reality. It's an opportunity for you to adjust your trajectory so that you can learn faster. Consequently, the more mistakes you make—and the faster you learn from them—the better.

How to speak from day one

To start speaking from the very beginning, you don't need to move overseas. In many cases, you can do so from the comfort of your home or while staying in your current city.

1. Find someone to talk to

The first step is to find a native speaker you can interact with. To do so, you can:

- Talk to a native speaker friend. If you know a native speaker of your target language, that's probably the best place to start. Contact them and see if you can arrange a meeting either online or offline.
- Find a language exchange partner. Alternatively, you can look for one. To find an exchange partner you can visit websites such as *Tandem, Conversation Exchange, My Language Exchange, HelloTalk* or *Speakly*. You can also search for relevant groups on social media platforms.
- Finally, you can look for teachers online. I recommend sites such as *Italki, Preply* or *Amazing Talker*.

2. Prepare for your first interaction

Learn a few basic sentences and words. Benny Lewis recommends we spend a couple of hours preparing. For instance, he suggests we study basic sentences such as:

- How are you?
- What's your name?
- My name is ...
- I don't understand.
- Could you repeat that?
- Can you speak slower, please?
- What does ***insert word or expression here*** mean?

3. Talk in your target language

Now, that you've found someone to talk to and have prepared in advance, you can connect via video messenger or meet in person. Try practicing what you learn without worrying too much. The point is just to get started.

Make sure you tell your exchange partner or teacher that you only want to speak in your target language (at least when practicing the few words and sentences you know). Your first conversation may not last long, but the key is to get started and develop the habit of speaking in your target language. It will be messy at first, but you'll make progress fairy quickly.

4. Rinse and repeat

You can then repeat the process with your teacher, exchange partner or friends. To do so, you can:

- **Learn what you're the most likely to use in the next session.** Instead of learning using a regular textbook, you can gear your learning toward specific topics you want to talk about in your practice conversations. This will help you make sure you have something to say during your conversations, thereby helping you to improve your speaking skills more quickly.
- **Write down a few words or expressions you want to use but didn't have time to memorize.** You may not have time to remember all the words or expressions you want to use. If so, write them down on a piece of paper or in a file on your

computer. Then, look at your notes whenever needed during your conversation.

- **Look things up during your conversation if necessary.** If you don't understand something, look it up using software like *Google Translate* or *Deepl*.

By following this process, you'll be able to speak from day one even if the language is completely new to you. Another added benefit is that you'll be gaining confidence as you realize that you can already speak a few words. Remember, many people wait months or even years before they try speaking, since they're afraid of making mistakes or of being judged.

2) Set specific goals

Learning a foreign language is easier when you have a well-defined goal that excites you. So, using what we talked about in the part "What you should learn", set a SMART goal that inspires you.

For instance, your goal could be to travel to a country where you'll be able to speak your target language. Making it specific could mean using that language in every store you visit there, or it could be having a conversation with a friend.

Another goal could be to watch your favorite movie dubbed into your target language, with the intention of understanding as much as possible.

Once you've set a goal, you can break it down into multiple milestones, and create a learning schedule to help you reach your goal. If needed, refer to the section on setting SMART goals.

3) Challenge yourself/have skin in the game

With direct learning, the point is to have skin in the game. It is to put yourself in situations where you're challenged and need to be hyper-focused. Stretching yourself this way will enable you to learn more quickly.

For instance, I have two lessons a week with my Estonian teacher. Every time, I try to make more complex sentences and use new words or expressions I've learned. Even if I feel as though I won't be able to say what I want to say or make the sentence I want to make, I give it a shot anyway. It's messy and I make a ridiculous number of mistakes, but it doesn't matter. I learn during the process.

Challenging yourself also means:

- Trying hard to guess what someone might be saying based on the context
- Remembering the words you learned, and practicing them even if you get it wrong
- Asking people to repeat what they said instead of giving up on understanding them, and
- Attempting to construct a difficult sentence

I'm always surprised at how many people do not try to understand, and merely give up. Your brain is a pattern recognition machine. If you try hard enough, you will spot more and more patterns, whether in language learning or in anything else in life. Therefore, always believe you can figure things out.

Assuming your goal is to have conversations, focus most of your effort on practicing speaking in your target language. You can focus on writing and reading later. As for listening, whenever you interact with a native speaker, you'll be practicing. As you keep interacting with native speakers, you'll learn most of the grammar naturally.

4) Make your goal a priority

Learning a foreign language requires time and effort. There is no way around that. Therefore, if you wish to make progress fast and reach a conversational level in a few months, spend as much time as possible learning and speaking your target language. The polyglot, Benny Lewis, recommends that we spend at least two hours a day, every day. This will be enough to make serious progress in a matter of months.

Now, if you can't spend that much time or don't want to, aim at thirty minutes a day. The key is to stay consistent over the long run.

5) Create a schedule

To make progress long term, you must create a specific schedule and stick to it. For instance, I decided to have a forty-five-minute Estonian lesson every Monday and Thursday from 6:30 pm to 7:15 pm. I also spend fifteen to thirty minutes daily learning Estonian using the app, *Speakly*.

Consistency is essential. To transfer your language skills to your subconscious, you must practice regularly. If you wait too long between study sessions, you'll forget too much, and won't be able to make fast enough progress to keep the momentum going and maintain motivation long term. Aim at studying a little every single day.

Concrete plan of action

Let's have a look at a concrete plan of action you can start using right away to learn a language. You can create your plan using your action guide.

1. **Select a target language.** Make sure that you're genuinely excited about learning that language. Remember, the more passionate you are, the better learner you will be.
2. **Set a clear goal.** Clearly define a specific goal you want to reach by a set date. For instance, it could be to talk about one of your hobbies in your target language. I recommend you set a ninety-day goal. Ninety days is long enough to achieve tangible results but short enough to force you to study seriously each day.
3. **Find someone you can speak with in that language.** Ask a native speaker friend, find an exchange partner or hire a teacher.
4. **Create a learning schedule.** When learning a language (or anything else) consistency is key. Make sure you practice daily. At a minimum, aim at studying at least thirty minutes a day, but two hours per day is better.
5. **Prepare for your first speaking session.** Learn basic words and expressions so that you can introduce yourself and say a

few words. You can also prepare a document with the words you want to say but didn't have time to remember.

6. **Have your first speaking session.** Speak in your target language while avoiding worrying about making mistakes. Just being able to say a few words from day one is a massive accomplishment that will boost your self-esteem. Pat yourself on your back when you're done!

7. **Practice speaking regularly.** Try to find someone you can talk to on a regular basis (at least a couple of times per week). This will ensure you make consistent progress.

8. **Focus on improving your speaking skills.** When studying by yourself, prepare for the next speaking session. Review the vocabulary you used previously and learn new vocabulary to use during your next conversation. Select topics you're interested in. This will keep you engaged while enabling you to improve your speaking abilities. You can also use *Anki* cards to learn new words each day and study grammar.

Bonus: In your free time, consume content in your target language. Reading articles or books, watching videos and listening to music or podcasts is a great way to improve your language skills. This is what the second language learning method we're going to talk about is mostly about.

As you improve, you can also spend more time studying grammar. You'll find it more interesting now that you understand a little more about how the language works.

* * *

Action step

In your action guide, create your ninety-day learning plan.

To learn about the direct learning method in greater depth, check out Benny Lewis' book, *Fluent in 3 Months*.

B. Input learning

The idea behind input learning is to expose yourself to as much content as possible by watching YouTube videos and movies, reading blogs and comic books, listening to podcasts, and so on. The point is to *acquire* a language rather than merely *learn* it. And to acquire a language, we must increase our exposure in a way that maximizes our comprehension.

This method is based on the input hypothesis as described by the linguist Stephen Krashen. His point is, *"We acquire language in one way, and only one way: when we understand messages."* And the best way to increase our understanding of a foreign language is to consume content we can comprehend. This is often referred to as "comprehensible input".

This method has gained popularity in recent years thanks to an American YouTuber, Matt vs. Japan, who used it to reach fluency in Japanese. Matt created a website called *Refold* in which he explains, in great detail, how to use the input learning method to reach fluency.

One key characteristic of this method is that you don't try to speak from day one. You first learn the most common words in your target language and listen to a load of content in that language (starting with simple content), while learning only the minimum grammar. It's only once you have acquired solid foundations that you begin to speak, which can take three to six months or more. The key point in this method is that you must understand first before trying to speak. You must acquire the essence of the language through repeated exposure rather than by immersing yourself in grammar books, or relying on more traditional learning methods.

Now, you can speak if you want, but to quote Stephen Krashen, "Speaking is not practicing." Speaking early on will not make a major difference in our ability to acquire a foreign language over time.

This method may sound counterintuitive. However, it's not that different from the way we learned when we were babies. Before we even pronounced a word, we already consumed a lot of content. It's also how Scandinavians learn to speak English, for the most part. Sure, language classes at school probably help. However, I suspect watching TV shows in English from an early age plays a much bigger role (in bigger countries like France, movies and TV shows are dubbed into French).

Here is what the YouTuber, JJsays, an American fluent in Chinese, said regarding this method:

"This has been changing my life. Honestly. Increasing my input and using Anki has honestly done wonders to me. I find myself repeating things in my everyday life that I didn't even realize I knew how to say. That actually never happened to me before. It never happened to me with traditional language study. It's like my brain is on steroids in terms of my ability to remember and recall things."

Before we explain how this method works and how you can get started in greater detail, let's see who will benefit the most from it.

Who is this method for?

The input learning method is geared toward people who aspire to reach a high level of fluency in the mid-to-long term. Because you don't practice speaking before you have acquired a certain level of understanding, you won't be able to have conversations in the first few months. However, by consuming content in your target language daily, you'll be able to acquire solid foundations and speak much more naturally once you enter the speaking phase later.

How to use the input learning method to learn a language

Now that we've briefly seen what the input learning method is and who it is for, let's discuss how you can implement it to reach fluency in any target language.

Put simply, in this method, you:

- Learn the most common words in your target language using flashcards (and the writing system when necessary)
- Study a little grammar each day to get a rough understanding of how the language works

- Boost your understanding by consuming content in a specific topic of interest, and
- Start speaking only once you reach a decent level of understanding

More specifically, it entails doing the following things:

1. Selecting a topic that interests you

To reach a high level of comprehension in your target language, reduce the scope of your learning. Don't try to understand every topic possible. Instead, focus on one topic you're interested in and keep consuming related content until you reach a good level of comprehension.

For instance, it's a good idea to start with TV shows that depict the daily life of a person or a family. Watching such shows will enable you to learn the most common words in your target language, but you can also focus on other areas of interest, whether it is cooking or sports. That's up to you. The key is to keep the process interesting and to stay consistent.

2. Consuming content daily (input)

You consume content in your target language daily, ideally for one or two hours a day. If that's not possible, start with thirty minutes a day or so and ramp it up as you develop.

3. Consuming the right content for you

To ensure the content you consume helps you acquire the language, find content matching your current level. You don't need to understand everything, but you do need to be able to pick up a few words or sentences. Otherwise, you'll get bored or discouraged. Remember, learning is about understanding messages. The more comprehensible you can make the material, the better. We'll see ways to do that later.

Generally speaking, when you first start learning a new language, you want to have as much context as possible. For instance, TV shows with a simple story (such as a love story) are easier to understand than podcasts. You see the actors in specific situations, which can help you grasp (or guess) what they could be saying. Over time, your brain will naturally learn new words and sentences. To further increase your understanding, watch shows using subtitles in your target language (e.g., a Spanish show with Spanish subtitles).

Obviously, the degree of difficulty will also vary based on the topic. For instance, a documentary on World War II will be much harder to grasp than a comedy or a love story.

To begin with, select simple topics. Then, remove the subtitles when you want to challenge yourself a little more. Once you feel as though you have mastered a topic (or want some novelty), move on to more complicated topics.

Tip: Try to avoid using subtitles in your native language. This will prevent you from focusing on what's actually said, which will inhibit your learning.

4. Moving to more challenging content

As your level of comprehension increases, you can start focusing on more challenging content such as podcasts, which have less context and are harder to understand. The point is to challenge yourself so that you keep improving your comprehension.

In parallel to watching content, you'll also be learning the most common words as well as a little grammar. Once you've developed a large enough vocabulary, it will become much easier to understand daily life conversations.

5. Making input comprehensible

The more you consume materials geared toward your current level of understanding (but a little challenging), the faster you'll acquire your target language.

The key is to maximize both the amount and the quality of the input you're exposed to. If you consume input only five minutes a day, it will take you forever to learn. If you watch only content far above your level of comprehension, it will significantly inhibit your progress.

Now, let's look at seven ways to increase your understanding.

1. **Consume content you can (somewhat) understand.** Aim at something that is a little challenging. For instance, instead of reading regular books, read books geared toward beginners. Search online for "graded readers + your target language". Alternatively, watch TV shows or cartoons for kids or YouTube channels with comprehensible inputs for beginners.
2. **Prioritize highly contextual content** (e.g., cookery shows, dramas, stories for kids with plenty of images, et cetera). The more context you receive, the easier it will be to understand the content. For instance, practical videos like cooking shows are great. When you start learning a language, the more you can infer just from watching the video/images, the better.
3. **Use subtitles in your target language.** When needed (and when possible), put subtitles in your target language. This way, you'll have audio, video and written input simultaneously. Over time, remove the subtitles as you become more comfortable with the content. Alternatively, read books while listening to the audio version.
4. **Watch content you've already watched in your native language.** Re-watch your favorite movies or series, but in your target language. Since you already know the story, you'll understand much more.
5. **Re-watch videos.** With the input learning method, you'll consume a lot of content. From time to time, go back to videos you've already watched. You'll notice how much progress you've made, and you might even pick up new words or expressions. You can also keep reviewing a video you didn't understand well the first time.
6. **Watch videos on a topic you know well.** The more you know about a topic, the easier it will be to understand it in your target language. As you familiarize yourself with the

vocabulary, over time, you might even be able to learn new material in your target language.

7. **Use apps.** Nowadays, there are many apps that can help you boost your comprehension. For instance, you can download the Chrome plugin *Language Reactor*. This plugin adds subtitles, a pop-up dictionary and other features and can be used on sites like Netflix or YouTube.

How to implement the input learning method

The main drawback of the input learning method is that it requires time to implement. The site *refold.la* explains how the method works in detail. In this section, I will give you a solid overview and a concrete action plan to help you get started with it right away.

To simplify, this method is nothing more than consuming comprehensible content daily, while memorizing a few words and learning a little grammar and pronunciation along the way.

There are several nuances and ways to optimize your learning, but as long as you keep consuming content every day consistently and try to understand it, you can't really go wrong. Over time, you can tweak the method and refine your approach to make it even more effective.

To implement the input method, you need to create:

- A learning environment, and
- A learning plan

With these two components in place, learning will become much easier.

1. Creating a learning environment

One of the biggest challenges with input learning is that you must gather relevant material. You need to have a lot of content ready, as you'll be consuming hours and hours of video content every week. Fortunately, you'll probably find most of what you need on YouTube. Once you've found relevant content, you must organize it effectively to facilitate your daily study.

a. Finding relevant content

When you begin, you need to start with simple videos that will enable you to learn a few words or sentences. As you understand a little more each time, you'll feel motivated to keep learning. Remember, learning a language takes a great deal of time and effort. Don't expect to understand daily conversations overnight.

Examples of relevant content for complete beginners might be:

- Simple stories read by native speakers
- TV shows created specifically for language learners (e.g., *Extras*, a sitcom for English, French, German or Spanish speakers)
- Cartoons for kids
- Graded books using simple words matching your current level of comprehension

A little more advanced content for beginners may be:

- Sitcoms or love stories (especially if they have subtitles in your target language)
- Any video on the topic of interest you choose to focus on

Yet more advanced content may be:

- Series you enjoy on Netflix
- Sitcoms and love stories without subtitles

Remember, the key with this method is to:

1. Consume lots of content in your target language, and
2. Make the process as enjoyable as possible while learning

If you don't find a piece of content engaging, look for something more enjoyable.

I've created a resource page with content you can start using today. I've included resources for the most commonly learned languages (Spanish, French, Italian, German, Russia, Japanese, Chinese and Korean). On this page you'll find:

- Free *Anki* decks with the most common words in each language so that you can learn new vocabulary easily every day.
- Curated YouTube videos organized by level of difficulty, so you can start immersing yourself today.
- Basic grammar videos you can watch daily.
- Pronunciation videos to familiarize yourself with specific sounds in your target language.
- A ninety-day study schedule you can print out and use to start your learning journey.

My goal is to help you become operational right away rather than having to study for hours how to implement the method (like I had to). As you start using this method, you can increase your understanding of the method and refine your approach by visiting the website refold.ca or their YouTube channel Refold.

Tips to consume content consistently

With input learning, the key is to consume content in your target language every day consistently over a long period of time. Learning a language is not a sprint; it's a marathon. When you consume content, you want it to be:

- **Comprehensible.** Generally, the more you understand the content, the easier it will be to stay engaged. So, look for content that's challenging, but not too challenging. Find a balance. Refer to the tips mentioned in the part on how to make content as comprehensible as possible.
- **Compelling.** You may understand the content very well, but if it doesn't pique your interest, you'll quickly get bored. Look for content you find interesting or entertaining.

The point is that you must find a balance between interesting and comprehensible content. On days when you have a lot of energy and motivation, try listening to more challenging content. Conversely, on days where you feel a little tired or less motivated, consume easier and or more compelling content. For instance, you may review videos you've watched before or put your favorite series on Netflix with subtitles in your target language. If it's still too much of a stretch, add subtitles in English.

Select the appropriate content based on your energy level and motivation each day (see graph below). Strive to stay engaged whenever possible. Otherwise, be entertained.

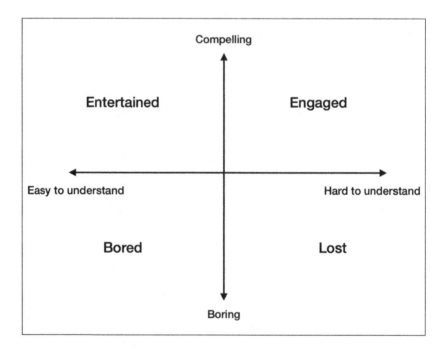

b. Gather grammar content

The next step is to find content you can use to study grammar. You can use textbooks, but I would recommend you look for videos, as they're likely to be more entertaining. Here, the goal is not to become a master of grammar nor to be able to explain how everything works and why. The goal is merely to build an understanding of the way the grammar works. Over time, your brain will connect the dots, and making sentences will become easier.

To find grammar content, look on YouTube for grammar videos. Prioritize bigger channels as it's often a sign their content is good. Look for playlists of grammar videos that go from basic to more advanced.

c. Gather the most common keywords

The greater your vocabulary, the more you'll be able to understand the content you consume. This is why you want to spend time learning at least five to ten words each day. By learning the top 1,000-2,000 most common words, you'll have a foundation that will enable you to understand more and more, giving you access to a larger panel of comprehensible input.

One of the best ways to learn new vocabulary is to use the app called Anki (free on desktop computers and Macs). Anki has a built-in SRS (spaced repetition system) and will show you words to maximize retention. You should create a deck of at least 1,000 words (or buy/download one). You can download free Anki decks on the resource page for this book.

d. Organize your content

To ensure you consume content every day, make it as easy as possible. I recommend keeping it simple by creating playlists on YouTube that you can access in a couple of clicks. You can also create a list of series or movies you want to watch on Netflix.

In addition, I encourage you to create a dedicated YouTube account for your target language. Look for the video entitled "How To: YouTube Immersion Accounts" on Youtube to learn how.

Having a dedicated YouTube account will provide you with more and more content suggestions. Over time, you'll only be shown relevant content in your target language. This is a smart way to make the YouTube algorithm work for you.

e. Gather pronunciation videos

Finally, find a website or some videos you can use to learn the correct pronunciation in your target language. You'll find pronunciation videos on the resource page.

Now that you've gathered learning materials, the next step is to implement a routine to help you stay consistent with your learning.

2. Creating a learning plan

We've already discussed how to create a learning plan, so I won't talk about it in too much depth here. The first thing to bear in mind is that with the input learning method, you need to have a long-term vision. If you aspire to become fluent in your target language, you'll probably need to spend one or two years (or more) studying every day or so.

How much time and for how long you'll need to study will depend on:

The language you're learning. The closer the language is to your mother tongue, the faster you'll acquire it. For instance, I've started studying Spanish and I can see that it's much, much easier than Japanese. That's because Spanish is very similar to French, my mother tongue. Yesterday, while going for a walk, I listened to videos from a Spanish YouTuber. Even though the video was entirely in Spanish, I was able to understand a lot. And that's only after studying with the input learning method for a few days.

The number of hours you consume content per week. How much progress you make depends largely on how many hours of content you consume providing that:

- 1. The content is adapted to your level
- 2. You do your best to understand it, and
- 3. You're engaged and interested in the content

The more you study, the faster you'll acquire your target language. Consequently, to make significant progress, aim at consuming content for one or two hours daily. It may sound a lot but, if you do it while cooking, driving, walking, exercising, washing the dishes and so on, it won't feel that way. This is especially true when you enjoy the content (which you should). Remember, most people spend hours each day on their phones, computers or sitting in front of the TV. You can do that but do it while watching content in your target language.

The number of study hours needed to reach fluency

Let's see how many hours you need, based on the difficulty of your target language. US Foreign Service Institute (FSI) has grouped world languages into four categories. I'll use their categories while providing what I believe are more realistic numbers to reach fluency for languages in each category.

- Level 1 (1,500 hours to fluency): this level includes romance languages such as Spanish, French, Italian and Portuguese as well as North Germanic languages such as Norwegian, Swedish, Danish and Dutch.
- Level 2 (2,000 hours to fluency): this includes German, Malay, Indonesian, Swahili or Haitian Creole.
- Level 3 (2,500 hours to fluency): this includes most of the other languages such as Slavic, Baltic, Indian, Uralic, Semitic, Hellenic languages, Armenian, Turkish, Thai, or Vietnamese.
- Level 4 (4,000-5,000 hours to fluency): this includes Arabic, Chinese, Japanese and Korean.

Here are a couple more things to consider:

- This is from the perspective of an English native speaker. For instance, if you're Japanese, you'll be able to learn somewhat similar languages such as Korean or Chinese faster than other languages.
- Once you've learned a language, you'll be able to acquire any new language faster than someone who has yet to master one foreign language.

Now let's see how to create a learning plan you can start using from today.

Create your ninety-day plan

Ninety days is just enough time to make tangible progress toward any major goal. This is why I recommend you create a ninety-day schedule for your language learning. You may not know exactly how much progress you'll make within ninety days, but that's fine. Goals are set to give you a direction and help you to put in place processes to follow each day.

To create your ninety-day plan, decide:

- How many words you'll learn each day (using Anki or other apps),
- The amount of time you'll spend studying each day,
- When exactly you'll be studying, and
- One specific goal you want to reach at the end of the ninety days.

To help you, print the ninety-day plan PDF available on the resources page.

To go further

After a few months studying with this method, you can create your own flashcards to learn more words. You can also practice various techniques such as shadowing, which entails repeating what you hear, trying to mimic pronunciation the best you can.

To learn more about the Refold method, check the roadmap on their website.

Main takeaways

The input learning method is based on the idea that we acquire a language by consuming content we can comprehend (comprehensible input).

To start implementing the input method, you need to:

- Decide on a target language
- Use flashcards to learn the 1,000-2000 most common words in that language
- Study a little grammar each day to help grasp how the language works
- Consume as much content as you can every day (ideally, at least one or two hours), and
- Start speaking only once you reach a decent level of understanding

To maximize your learning, try to find content that matches your current level or make existing content more comprehensible by:

- Prioritizing content that provides a lot of context
- Using subtitles in your target language
- Watching content that you've already watched in your native language
- Watching videos that you've watched before
- Watching videos on a topic you know well, and
- Using various apps

* * *

Action step

- Create your ninety-day plan using your action guide
- Check out the resources pack to help you get started

4

STANDARDIZED TESTS

Another type of learning is test-related learning. In this section, we'll cover specific techniques you can use for standardized tests such as language tests (TOEFL, Japanese language proficiency tests, et cetera) or academic tests (GMAT or school admission tests). In other words, any test that has a defined curriculum.

Luckily, I've never failed any standardized tests, whether it is TOEFL (English language test), GMAT (Graduate Management Admission Test), JLPT level one (the most advanced level of the Japanese Language Proficiency Test), or TOPIK (Intermediate level of the Test of Proficiency in Korean). So, hopefully, I can share effective methods to ensure that you also perform well at such tests.

Below are the key characteristics of standardized tests:

- Requires that you learn a specific curriculum
- Entails you acquire a well-defined set of skills or knowledge, and
- Usually demand that you rely more on declarative learning than procedural (though this may vary based on the type of test you're taking)

The good thing with standardized tests

One of the main characteristics of standardized tests is that there are usually very clear expectations that participants must meet to pass such tests. This is good news, because it means that, by understanding what's required of you, you can dramatically increase your chances of success.

Another good thing is that, with standardized tests, you usually have a specific deadline. For instance, when I took level two of the JLPT, the exam was only held once a year, so I had both a clear deadline and a strong incentive to prepare well for it. Deadlines are powerful. Standardized tests will impose a deadline on you. Make the most of it.

Now, let's look at effective ways to prepare for standardized tests in detail.

A. Identify what's expected of you

The first step is to make sure you understand exactly what's expected of you. Ask the following questions:

* What's the scope of the test?
* What are the different sections and what type of questions are they made of?
* What exactly are you required to understand?

For instance, for the JLPT, you need to know a certain numbers of words and Kanji (Chinese characters). There are also a set number of grammatical forms to learn. Then, there are reading and listening exercises, which students should be able to complete once they know the vocabulary and grammar, and have read and listened to enough material in Japanese.

B. Ask the advice of people who passed the exam before you

If there are effective learning techniques, you might want to know them. When I prepared for the GMAT—a test required to join an

MBA—I had a friend who had just joined a business school and he sold me all the textbooks he used when preparing for the exam.

You can also run a quick online search to identify what may be the best ways to approach learning for a specific exam.

C. Gather relevant learning material

The next step is to make sure you gather the best and most relevant learning material to prepare for the exam.

When I prepared for the JLPT, I made sure to buy all the official and unofficial textbooks I could find. I had:

- A grammar textbook that included all the grammatical forms with several examples for each—it also came with a CD to help increase my listening skills
- A vocabulary textbook covering all the words and Japanese characters included in the exam
- A textbook for reading comprehension with mock-up questions, and
- A book that included several past exams

In other words, I had textbooks covering each part of the exam alongside mock exams to assess my progress over time.

Similarly, when I prepared for the GMAT, I bought close to a dozen books, including *The Official Guide for GMAT Review*, an 840-page manual with over 800 past GMATs. Each book covered a specific part of the exam such as critical reasoning, sentence correction or quantitative review.

D. Create a learning schedule

Preparing for exams can take months or years. The only way you'll be able to stay consistent and study regularly is to create a specific learning schedule.

When I studied for the GMAT, I gave myself a specific amount of time to prepare for it. I must admit, I don't remember exactly how long the preparation took, but it was several months.

Set a deadline/register for the exam

More specifically, you need to set a deadline and possibly register for the exam. Some exams can only be taken once or twice a year, so you'll know what to expect. Other exams, like the GMAT or TOEFL, can be taken multiple times a year. However, I don't recommend you just register for an exam and take it, hoping for the best. Prepare as much as possible and register with the firm intent of passing it first time.

Create a schedule

Once you have set a deadline and/or have registered for the exam, you need to create a schedule. For example, when I studied for the GMAT, I had a full-time job, so I had to create a learning schedule around it.

- I studied in the morning before going to work for forty-five to sixty minutes
- I studied during my lunch break for forty-five minutes
- I studied during weekends from 10 am to 12am

I stuck to this schedule until it became a habit.

E. Assess where you stand

Before you get started with your study, it's often beneficial to assess how far away you are from reaching your goals. This will help you determine how much time and effort you need to put into your learning.

Let's say you want to go to business school and need to take the GMAT. If so, before you start studying, it's a good idea to take a mock exam. You may find out that the math part comes fairly easily, while the verbal reasoning part is quite challenging, or vice versa.

For instance, when I took a mock exam for the GMAT, I immediately realized that math was my biggest weakness, while verbal reasoning was my strength. Subsequently, I spent significantly more time trying to improve my math skills.

Now, if you happen to study for an exam for which you have no prior knowledge whatsoever, there is probably no need to take a mock exam at the beginning. Instead, wait until you have studied enough before taking your first mock exam.

F. Practice, practice, practice

Once you have created a learning schedule and identified your current level of skill, it's time to sit down and study.

When it comes to standardized tests, the key is to practice answering as many actual exam questions as possible. The best way to do so is to get ahold of exam questions from previous years (like The Official Guide for GMAT Review I mentioned earlier). Being confronted with real questions and learning to answer them correctly will allow you to perform well on the day of the exam. Consequently, find as many past exam questions as you can. If there are several books including such questions, consider buying as many as you need.

Use interleaved practice

As you study for your exam, alternate between problem types rather than focusing on answering questions of the same type before moving to another section/type of problem.

In his book, *Make it Stick*, Peter C. Brown shares a study in which two groups of college students practiced the same math problems (four problem types in total). The first group worked on four problems of the same type, before moving on to the next type. Meanwhile, the second group worked on the same problems, but the questions were mixed. When they were tested a week later, students in the first group only correctly answered twenty percent of the time, while students in the second group correctly answered sixty-three percent of the time.

The point is, design your study sessions to alternate between various type of problems. This will boost your learning and increase retention.

Learn from your mistakes

Now, don't simply go through the questions, do your best to answer them, and move on. Instead, identify all the questions you couldn't answer well. Then, take another shot at them until you answer correctly.

For instance, you can use the following technique:

- Write down the questions you answered wrong in your notebook so that you can refer to them later (write the section, page number and question number)
- Look at the correct answers, and
- Try answering the questions again in a couple of days

Alternatively:

- Write down the questions in your notebook
- Do not look at the answers, and
- Try to answer them in a few days

The key is to spend enough time on the questions you struggle to answer. There is no point answering easy questions repeatedly. This won't lead to optimal results.

G. Measure your progress

Great. You've now spent a few weeks studying for the exam, but how much progress have you really made? The only way to find out is to test yourself by taking a mock exam. This will:

- Help you identify your weak points and spot trends. Are you stagnating in certain areas? Are you making massive progress in others? Or are you regressing?
- Replicate exam conditions including time constraints and actual questions. This will prepare you mentally for the real exam.
- Give you invaluable feedback to improve your study techniques. For instance, you may discover that you're

spending too much time on certain types of questions. Or, you may discover that it is useful to start with certain sections and leave others for later.

For many standardized tests, you'll be able to find mock exams that closely mimic the actual test. When this is not possible, reflect on ways you could simulate the real exam. Perhaps you can put questions together or invite friends to help you with sections that may require human interaction.

Now, let's answer some questions you may have regarding mock exams.

How often should you take mock exams?

As we've seen, the goal of mock exams is to help you measure your progress and give you feedback, while preparing you mentally for the actual test. Therefore, there is no point in taking mock exams too often. You must give yourself enough time to improve before taking another mock exam. Consider taking one every month or two.

Should you take a complete mock exam or a partial one?

Do you really need to sit down for hours to take a full mock exam, or can you take a shorter version?

Here is what I recommend:

- Take three to five mock exams max before taking the actual exam. Taking mock exams requires time and effort. Don't take too many or you'll use up too much study time. Take one at the beginning, a couple more as you keep studying, and a final mock test a couple of weeks before the actual exam.
- Take partial mock exams whenever needed. To practice effectively on a specific section of your exam, take a partial mock exam for that section only. For example, as you study for the GMAT, you could spend one study session on "quantitative reasoning" only (sixty-two minutes and thirty-one questions).

H. Adjust your learning

Finally, after each mock exam, ask yourself whether you need to make an adjustment to your learning schedule. Dedicate more time and effort to certain sections or questions you're struggling with the most. Think of ways to improve your performance. Ask friends or mentors for study tips and so on.

There are no guarantees but following these steps will offer you the best chance of passing whatever standard exam you are applying for.

Main takeaways

- **Identify what's expected of you.** Make sure you know exactly what you need to learn to pass the exam. These requirements are usually specific and finite.
- **Ask the advice of people who have already passed the exam.** Find people who have passed the exams before and ask for advice. Do a quick search online to identify the best way to prepare for the exam.
- **Gather relevant learning materials.** Get your hands on all the official and unofficial guides and other relevant materials. Gather as many sample questions from previous exams as you can find.
- **Create a learning schedule.** Decide how long you have available to prepare for the exam and/or register for the exam when necessary. Then, create a daily or weekly routine to ensure you're making consistent progress.
- **Assess where you are.** Take a mock exam at the beginning to identify the areas on which you need to spend more time. Then, make sure you reflect the results in your learning schedule.
- **Practice, practice, practice.** As part of your study sessions, answer as many actual questions from previous exams as you can. Make sure to learn from your mistakes. To do so, take note of questions you couldn't answer correctly, and test yourself a few days later (after studying the relevant topic).

Dedicate more time to sections of the exam you're struggling with the most.

- **Measure your progress.** Take mock exams every four to eight weeks. This will prepare you mentally by putting you in exam-like situations. It will also enable you to spot areas in need of improvement as well as give you hints on how to perform better during the actual test. In addition, take partial mock tests as often as needed to measure your progress at a more granular level.
- **Adjust your learning.** Finally, see whether you need to make an adjustment to your learning plan based on the results from the mock tests. Dedicate more time to questions you're struggling with or critical parts that account for a significant portion of the final grade.

CONCLUSION

As the world becomes more and more complex, your ability to learn faster and better than most people will give you an incredible advantage, and will allow you to reach almost any goal you set. Remember, learning is the process that enables you to move from where you are to where you wish to be.

As we've seen in this book, the great news is that learning is an inevitable process. When you develop the proper mindset, build the identity of a learner, define what you want to learn and why, and use effective learning techniques, you will *inevitably* move closer to your goals.

You will sometimes doubt yourself. When this happens, remember that learning can be a chaotic process with its peaks and valleys. Progress may be slower than you expect. However, as you create effective processes and stick to your goals, you'll eventually be able to learn new skills and acquire more knowledge. The key is to stay focused and avoid biting off more than you can chew. To do so, select a few goals that genuinely inspire you, implement the best blueprint possible and keep going until you reach your target. Once you know how to reach one goal, you'll be able to replicate the same process over and over for anything else you desire to learn.

Also, as you keep learning, have fun. Learn what *you* want to learn, not what you *think* you should learn or what others want you to learn. Being passionate is the most powerful learning technique available. You can do pretty much everything else wrong, but if you love what you do, you'll acquire even the most complicated skills and master the most obscure of subjects.

Now, let's be honest. You will not be able to absorb the entire content of this book in just one reading. You will not apply everything perfectly, and neither do you need to. The key is to become more deliberate with what you choose to learn, and how you learn it. By reading and rereading this book, and making incremental progress over time, you'll develop a powerful learning mindset and master some of the most effective learning techniques. This will make you a far better learner.

To conclude, let me remind you that you are smart enough to figure things out. Never let people tell you that something is too complicated for you, or that you can't learn a specific skill or discipline. If many people have learned the subject before you, you can too.

Remember, you can always learn, grow and improve. You can figure things out. Learning is inevitable, and as you master the process, you'll be able to learn better and faster than almost anybody else. That will become your superpower.

What do you think?

I hope you benefit from this book. I would be very grateful if you could take a moment to leave an honest review on Amazon.

Thanks again for your support!

Thibaut

MASTER YOUR EMOTIONS (PREVIEW)

 The mind is its own place, and in itself can make a heaven of Hell, a hell of Heaven.

— JOHN MILTON, POET.

We all experience a wide range of emotions throughout our lives. I had to admit, while writing this book, I experienced highs and lows myself. At first, I was filled with excitement and thrilled at the idea of providing people with a guide to help them understand their emotions. I imagined how readers' lives would improve as they learned to control their emotions. My motivation was high and I couldn't help but imagine how great the book would be.

Or so I thought.

After the initial excitement, the time came to sit down to write the actual book, and that's when the excitement wore off pretty quickly. Suddenly ideas that looked great in my mind felt dull. My writing seemed boring, and I felt as though I had nothing substantive or valuable to contribute.

Sitting at my desk and writing became more challenging each day. I started losing confidence. Who was I to write a book about emotions if I couldn't even master my own emotions? How ironic! I considered giving up. There are already plenty of books on the topic, so why add one more?

At the same time, I realized this book was a perfect opportunity to work on my emotional issues. And who doesn't suffer from negative emotions from time to time? We all have highs and lows, don't we? The key is what we *do* with our lows. Are we using our emotions to grow and learn or are we beating ourselves up over them?

So, let's talk about *your* emotions now. Let me start by asking you this:

How do you feel right now?

Knowing how you feel is the first step toward taking control of your emotions. You may have spent so much time internalizing you've lost touch with your feelings. Perhaps you answered as follows: "I feel this book could be useful," or "I really feel I could learn something from this book."

However, none of these answers reflect on how you feel. You don't 'feel like this,' or 'feel like that,' you simply 'feel.' You don't 'feel like' this book could be useful, you 'think' this book could be useful, and that generates an emotion which makes you 'feel' excited about reading it. Feelings manifest as physical sensations in your body, not as an idea in your mind. Perhaps, the reason the word 'feel' is so often overused or misused is because we don't want to talk about our emotions.

So, how do you feel now?

Why is it important to talk about emotions?

How you feel determines the quality of your life. Your emotions can make your life miserable or truly magical. That's why they are among the most essential things on which to focus. Your emotions color all your experiences. When you feel good, everything seems, feels, or tastes better. You also think better thoughts. Your energy levels are higher and possibilities seem limitless. Conversely, when you feel depressed, everything seems dull. You have little energy and you become unmotivated. You feel stuck in a place (mentally and physically) you don't want to be, and the future looks gloomy.

Your emotions can also act as a powerful guide. They can tell you something is wrong and allow you to make changes in your life. As such, they may be among the most powerful personal growth tools you have.

Sadly, neither your teachers nor your parents taught you how emotions work or how to control them. I find it ironic that just about anything comes with a how-to manual, while your mind doesn't. You've never received an instruction manual to teach you how your mind works and how to use it to better manage your emotions, have you? I haven't. In fact, until now, I doubt one even existed.

What you'll learn in this book

This book is the how-to manual your parents should have given you at birth. It's the instruction manual you should have received at school. In it, I'll share everything you need to know about emotions so you can overcome your fears and limitations and become the type of person you want to be.

More specifically, this book will help you:

- Understand what emotions are and how they impact your life
- Understand how emotions form and how you can use them for your personal growth
- Identify negative emotions that control your life and learn to overcome them
- Change your story to take better control over your life and create a more compelling future,
- Reprogram your mind to experience more positive emotions.
- Deal with negative emotions and condition your mind to create more positive ones

- Gain all the tools you need to start recognizing and controlling your emotions

Here is a more detailed summary of what you'll learn in this book:

In **Part I**, we'll discuss what emotions are. You'll learn why your brain is wired to focus on negativity and what you can do to counter this effect. You'll also discover how your beliefs impinge upon your emotions. Finally, you'll learn how negative emotions work and why they are so tricky.

In **Part II**, we'll go over the things that directly impact your emotions. You'll understand the roles your body, your thoughts, your words, or your sleep, play in your life and how you can use them to change your emotions.

In **Part III**, you'll learn how emotions form and how to condition your mind to experience more positive emotions.

And finally, in **Part IV**, we'll discuss how to use your emotions as a tool for personal growth. You'll learn why you experience emotions such as fear or depression and how they work.

Let's get started.

To start mastering your emotions today go to

mybook.to/Master_Emotions

I. What emotions are

Have you ever wondered what emotions are and what purpose they serve?

In this section, we'll discuss how your survival mechanism affects your emotions. Then, we'll explain what the 'ego' is and how it impacts your emotions. Finally, we'll discover the mechanism behind emotions and learn why it can be so hard to deal with negative ones.

Why people have a bias towards negativity

Your brain is designed for survival, which explains why you're able to read this book at this very moment. When you think about it, the probability of you being born was extremely low. For this miracle to happen, all the generations before you had to survive long enough to procreate. In their quest for survival and procreation, they must have faced death hundreds or perhaps thousands of times.

Fortunately, unlike your ancestors, you're (probably) not facing death every day. In fact, in many parts of the world, life has never been safer. Yet, your survival mechanism hasn't changed much. Your brain still scans your environment looking for potential threats.

In many ways, some parts of your brain have become obsolete. While you may not be seconds away from being eaten by a predator, your brain still gives significantly more weight to adverse events than to positive ones.

Fear of rejection is one example of a bias toward negativity. In the past, being rejected by your tribe would reduce your chances of survival significantly. Therefore, you learned to look for any sign of rejection, and this became hardwired in your brain.

Nowadays, being rejected often carries little or no consequence to your long-term survival. You can be hated by the entire world and still have a job, a roof and plenty of food on the table, yet, your brain remains programmed to perceive rejection as a threat to your survival.

This hardwiring is why rejection can be so painful. While you know most rejections are no big deal, you nevertheless feel the emotional pain. If you listen to your mind, you may even create a whole drama around it. You may believe you aren't worthy of love and dwell on a rejection for days or weeks. Worse still, you may become depressed as a result of this rejection.

One single criticism can often outweigh hundreds of positive ones. That's why, an author with fifty 5-star reviews, is likely to feel terrible when they receive a single 1-star review. While the author understands the 1-star review isn't a threat to her survival, her authorial brain doesn't. It likely interprets the negative review as a threat to her ego which triggers an emotional reaction.

The fear of rejection can also lead you to over-dramatize events. If your boss criticized you at work, your brain might see the criticism as a threat and you now think, "What if my boss fires me? What if I can't find a job quickly enough and my wife leaves me? What about my kids? What if I can't see them again?"

While you are fortunate to have such a useful survival mechanism, it is also your responsibility to separate real threats from imaginary ones. If you don't, you'll experience unnecessary pain and worry that will negatively impact the quality of your life. To overcome this bias towards negativity, you must reprogram your mind. One of a human being's greatest powers is our ability to use our thoughts to shape our reality and interpret events in a more empowering way. This book will teach you how to do this.

Why your brain's job isn't to make you happy

Your brain's primary responsibility is not to make you happy, but to ensure your survival. Thus, if you want to be happy, you must actively take control of your emotions rather than hoping you'll be happy because it's your natural state. In the following section, we'll discuss what happiness is and how it works.

How dopamine can mess with your happiness

Dopamine is a neurotransmitter that, among other functions, plays a significant role in rewarding certain behaviors. When dopamine releases into specific areas of your brain—the pleasure centers—you get an intense sense of wellbeing similar to a high. This sense of wellbeing is what happens during exercise, when you gamble, have sex, or eat great food.

One of the roles of dopamine is to ensure you look for food so you don't die of starvation, and you search for a mate so you can reproduce. Without dopamine, our species would likely be extinct by now. It's a pretty good thing, right?

Well, yes and no. In today's world, this reward system is, in many cases, obsolete. In the past, dopamine directly linked to our survival, now, it can be stimulated artificially. A great example of this effect is social media, which uses psychology to suck as much time as possible out of your life. Have you noticed all these notifications that pop up regularly? They're used to trigger a release of dopamine so you stay connected, and the longer you stay connected, the more money the services make. Watching pornography or gambling also leads to a release of dopamine which can make these activities highly addictive.

Fortunately, we don't need to act each time our brain releases dopamine. For instance, we don't need to continuously check our Facebook newsfeeds just because it gives us a pleasurable shot of dopamine.

Today's society is selling a version of happiness that can make us *un*happy. We've become addicted to dopamine mainly because of marketers who have found effective ways to exploit our brains. We receive multiple shots of dopamine throughout the day and we love it. But is that the same thing as happiness?

Worse than that, dopamine can create real addictions with severe consequences on our health. Research conducted at Tulane University showed that, when permitted to self-stimulate their pleasure center, participants did it an average of forty times per minute. They chose the stimulation of their pleasure center over food, even refusing to eat when hungry!

Korean, Lee Seung Seop is an extreme case of this syndrome. In 2005, Mr Seop died after playing a video game for fifty-eight hours straight with very little food or water, and no sleep. The subsequent investigation concluded the cause of death was heart failure induced by exhaustion and dehydration. He was only twenty-eight years old.

To take control of your emotions, you must understand the role dopamine plays and how it affects your happiness. Are you addicted to your phone? Are you glued to your TV? Or maybe you spend too much time playing video games. Most of us are addicted to something. For some people it's obvious, but for others, it's more subtle. For instance, you could be addicted to thinking. To better control your emotions, you must recognize and shed the light on your addictions as they can rob you of your happiness.

The 'one day I will' myth

Do you believe that one day you will achieve your dream and finally be happy? It is unlikely to happen. You may (and I hope you will) achieve your goal, but you won't live 'happily ever after.' This thinking is just another trick your mind plays on you.

Your mind quickly acclimates to new situations, which is probably the result of evolution and our need to adapt continually to survive and reproduce. This acclimatization is also probably why the new car or house you want will only make you happy for a while. Once the initial excitement wears off, you'll move on to crave the next exciting thing. This phenomenon is known as 'hedonic adaptation.'

How hedonic adaptation works

Let me share an interesting study that will likely change the way you see happiness. This study, which was conducted in 1978 on lottery winners and paraplegics, was incredibly eye-opening for me. The investigation evaluated how winning the lottery or becoming a paraplegic influence happiness:

The study found that one year after the event, both groups were just as happy as they were beforehand. Yes, just as happy (or unhappy). You can find more about it by watching Dan Gilbert's TED Talk, The Surprising Science of Happiness.

Perhaps you believe that you'll be happy once you've 'made it.' But, as the above study on happiness shows, this is simply not true. No matter what happens to you, your mind works by reverting to your predetermined level of happiness once you've adapted to the new event.

Does that mean you can't be happier than you are right now? No. What it means is that, in the long run, external events have minimal impact on your level of happiness.

In fact, according to Sonja Lyubomirsky, author of *The How of Happiness*, fifty percent of our happiness is determined by genetics, forty percent by internal factors, and only ten percent by external factors. These external factors include such things as whether we're single or married, rich or poor, and similar social influences.

The influence of external factors is probably way less than you thought. The bottom line is this: Your attitude towards life influences your happiness, not what happens to you.

By now, you understand how your survival mechanism negatively impacts your emotions and prevents you from experiencing more joy and happiness in your life. In the next section, we'll learn about the ego.

To read more visit my author page at:

amazon.com/author/thibautmeurisse

OTHER BOOKS BY THE AUTHORS:

Mastery Series

1. Master Your Emotions: A Practical Guide to Overcome Negativity and Better Manage Your Feelings

2. Master Your Motivation: A Practical Guide to Unstick Yourself, Build Momentum and Sustain Long-Term Motivation

3. Master Your Focus: A Practical Guide to Stop Chasing the Next Thing and Focus on What Matters Until It's Done

4. Master Your Destiny: A Practical Guide to Rewrite Your Story and Become the Person You Want to Be

5. Master Your Thinking: A Practical Guide to Align Yourself with Reality and Achieve Tangible Results in the Real World

6. Master Your Success: Timeless Principles to Develop Inner Confidence and Create Authentic Success

7. Master Your Beliefs: A Practical Guide to Stop Doubting Yourself and Build Unshakeable Confidence

8. Master Your Time: A Practical Guide to Increase Your Productivity and Use Your Time Meaningfully

Productivity Series

1. Dopamine Detox: A Short Guide to Remove Distractions and Get Your Brain to Do Hard Things

2. Immediate Action: A 7-Day Plan to Overcome Procrastination and Regain Your Motivation

3. Powerful Focus: A 7-Day Plan to Develop Mental Clarity and Build Strong Focus

4. Strategic Mindset: A 7-Day Plan to Identify What Matters and Create a Strategy that Works

Other books

Crush Your Limits: Break Free from Limitations and Achieve Your True Potential

Goal Setting: The Ultimate Guide to Achieving Life-Changing Goals

Habits That Stick: The Ultimate Guide to Building Habits That Stick Once and For All

Productivity Beast: An Unconventional Guide to Getting Things Done

The Greatness Manifesto: Overcome Your Fear and Go After What You Really Want

The One Goal: Master the Art of Goal Setting, Win Your Inner Battles, and Achieve Exceptional Results

The Passion Manifesto: Escape the Rat Race, Uncover Your Passion and Design a Career and Life You Love

The Thriving Introvert: Embrace the Gift of Introversion and Live the Life You Were Meant to Live

The Ultimate Goal Setting Planner: Become an Unstoppable Goal Achiever in 90 Days or Less

Upgrade Yourself: Simple Strategies to Transform Your Mindset, Improve Your Habits and Change Your Life

Success is Inevitable: 17 Laws to Unlock Your Hidden Potential, Skyrocket Your Confidence and Get What You Want From Life

Wake Up Call: How To Take Control Of Your Morning And Transform Your Life

ABOUT THE AUTHOR

THIBAUT MEURISSE

Thibaut Meurisse is a personal development blogger, author, and founder of whatispersonaldevelopment.org. M

Obsessed with self-improvement and fascinated by the power of the brain, his personal mission is to help people realize their full potential and reach higher levels of fulfillment and consciousness.

In love with foreign languages, he is French, writes in English, and lived in Japan for almost ten years.

Learn more about Thibaut at:

amazon.com/author/thibautmeurisse
whatispersonaldevelopment.org
thibaut.meurisse@gmail.com

Step-by-Step
Workbook

Part I. Building Solid Learning Roots

Six common learning issues

Issue #1—You try to learn too much

Write at least one specific time when you took on more than you could handle.

Issue #2—You're overly passive with your learning

Write down two to three concrete things you can start doing to become a more proactive learner.

Issue #3—There is no clear purpose behind your learning

In the space below, list all the things you genuinely want to learn, not because you need to, or because you want to impress others, but because they really interest you.

Issue #4—You're not taking enough action

Write down what taking more action would mean for you when it comes to learning.

Issue #5—You lack confidence in your ability to learn

If you could learn absolutely anything you desire, what would it be? Write down your answer below.

Issue #6—You have unrealistic expectations

Write down specific situations when you fell for the illusion of knowing. In other words, write down things you don't know as well as you think.

Developing a learning mindset

A. Shift your identity

See yourself as a highly effective learner. To start building your new identity, complete the following sentences below. Create five to ten statements.

I'm an unstoppable learner, therefore I:

_____

_____

_____

_____

B. Adopt a growth mindset

Familiarize yourself with the following statements:

- I embrace challenges.
- I always persist in the face of obstacles.
- I see effort as the necessary path to mastery.
- I accept constructive criticism.
- I learn from the success of others.

Think of a goal you're pursuing right now. Then, on the spaces provided, write down concretely what it would mean for you to adopt a growth mindset to reach that goal.

C. Understand the power of neuroplasticity

You're not too old to reach your goals. Write down one thing you've always wanted to do but gave up on because you considered yourself too old (or for other reasons).

Now, knowing that your brain is malleable and adaptable to change, what could you do to make progress toward that goal?

D. Adopt empowering beliefs about learning

Complete the following statements below and start building your new identity:

I can always learn and grow because_____

I can figure things out because_____

Learning is an inevitable process because_____

I can learn faster than almost anybody else because_____

_____

E. Master the learning process

Write down a goal you failed to reach in the past. Then, write down what you would do differently if you were to start all over again (now you know about the learning cycle).

Your goals:

What would you do differently:

F. Make your subconscious work for you

Write down how you will make your subconscious work for you.

What should you learn?

The different levels of skills

Using the table below, write down all the skills you're currently learning. Separate them into minor, intermediate, and major skills. Then, assess whether you're spending enough time on major skills.

#	Minor skills	Intermediate skills	Major skills
1			
2			
3			
4			
5			
6			
7			
8			
9			
10			

Identifying your learning goals

A. Selecting your learning goals

Brainstorm things you want to learn in the future. Just write down what comes to mind. For now, don't worry whether you want to start learning them tomorrow or in a decade, and don't even worry whether you'll actually learn them.

Fill in the table below:

Things you want to learn	Level of interest (on a scale from 1 to 10	Usefulness (on a scale from 1 to 10)	Relevancy right now (on a scale from 1 to 10)

Now, identify the two or three skills that gathered the most points in the table. These are the skills you should focus on right now. Don't blindly follow this formula though. Ask yourself how you feel about these skills. What is your intuition telling you? Which skill(s) on your list are you the most excited about?

B. Specifying your learning goals

1) Visualizing the result

Select one skill you'd like to learn. Then, answer the following questions:

What do you want to learn?

What do you want to be able to do?

What level of proficiency do you want to reach?

What future "memories" do you want your new skill to help you create?

2) Strengthening your "whys"

- Returning to the goal you selected in the previous exercise, write down ten reasons why you *must* absolutely reach that goal.
- Then, write down the three to five most important core values you aspire to live by.

Why I *must* reach that goal

1. _____

2. _____

3. _____

4. _____

5. _____

6. _____

7. _____

8. _____

9. _____

10. _____

My three core values:

1. _____

2. _____

3. _____

3) Creating the best action plan possible

Using the previous goal, reflect on your current blueprint. Is it the best strategy possible? If not, what could you do to find or create a more effective blueprint? Write your answer below.

4) Identifying process and result goals

Look at your previous goal. Then, determine the best process and results goals for it. Write them down below.

Process goals:

Results goals:

5) Making your goals SMART

Create your **SMART** learning goal.

- Specific
- Measurable
- Achievable
- Relevant
- Time-bound.

Your SMART goal:

6) Chunking down your goals

What could you do specifically to break your goal down into manageable tasks? Write down your answers below.

Implementing your plan

Write down your answers to the questions below.

How much time you can spend on your goal every week realistically.

When you'll be working on the learning goal you've already identified.

One thing you could do to help you stay on track with your learning goals over the long term (i.e., hiring a coach or having an accountability partner).

Part II. Strengthening Your Learning Tree Trunk

Come up with your own definitions of economics and politics. Do not spend more than ten to fifteen minutes doing so. And do not consult a dictionary before you have written down your own definition.

Part III. Watering Your Tree

Come up with specific examples to illustrate a new concept. To go further, create your own examples from your personal life or from the life of people you know. When necessary, make up examples.

Part IV. Pruning The Tree

Overcoming information overload

Elaborate below:

The type of information you consume during a typical week.

What you'll do specifically to reduce the amount of information you consume.

Part V. The Different Types of Learning

1. Conceptual Learning

For conceptual learning, you can apply most of the effective learning techniques mentioned in the book, such as recalling, elaborating, or spaced repetition.

To reiterate, below are also a few tips on learning conceptual skills:

1. **Master the fundamentals** and build solid learning foundations.
2. **Go from general to specific.** Don't be overwhelmed by the sea of information as you learn, and seek to deepen your understanding in the field you seek to build expertise in.
3. **Start with accessible content.** Instead of jumping into books and expert articles, start with the simplest and readily available content you can find.
4. **Look for specific examples.** This can help deepen your understanding, and allow you to build a good mental representation of a concept or idea.
5. **Come up with your own examples.** A sign that you truly understood something is your ability to simplify an idea by providing your own explanations and examples.
6. **Expand your personal library of mental models.** Mental models give you a bigger receptacle to hold more knowledge.
7. **Use the Feynman Technique.** Or simply put – write. Writing allows you to sharpen your thinking, and make you a better learner in the process.

2. Practical Skills

How to practice deliberately

Write down what deliberate practice would look like specifically for one of your goals.

Your goal:

What deliberate practice you will implement:

3. Language Learning

A. Direct Learning

1) Speak from day one

2) Set specific goals

3) Challenge yourself/have skin in the game

4) Make your goal a priority

5) Create a schedule

In the space provided, create your ninety-day learning plan.

My ninety-day learning plan.

B. Input learning

Create your ninety-day plan. To create your ninety-day plan decide:

- How many words you'll learn each day (using Anki or other apps),
- The amount of time you'll spend studying each day,
- When exactly you'll be studying, and
- One specific goal you want to reach at the end of the ninety days.

4. Standardized Tests

Standardized tests usually have clear expectations of you in order to pass, and deadlines to meet – which pushes you to study and prepare well.

Effective ways to prepare for standardized tests:

1. Identify what's expected of you.
2. Ask the advice from people who went through a similar test.
3. Gather relevant learning material.
4. Create a learning schedule.
5. Assess where you stand.
6. Practice.
7. Measure your progress.
8. Adjust your learning.

Additional notes:

Additional notes:

Additional notes:

Made in the USA
Las Vegas, NV
13 March 2024

87126577R00144